TRAVELING THE NATCHEZ TRACE

OTHER BOOKS BY LORI FINLEY

*Mountain Biking the Appalachians: Brevard-Asheville/
The Pisgah Forest*

Mountain Biking the Appalachians: Highlands-Cashiers

*Mountain Biking the Appalachians:
Northwest North Carolina/Southwest Virginia*

The Mountain Biker's Guide to the Southeast
(Menasha Ridge Press/ Falcon Press)

Traveling the Natchez Trace

by Lori Finley

® John F. Blair, Publisher • *Winston-Salem, North Carolina*

Second Printing, 1997

MAPS BY DEBRA LONG HAMPTON
PRINTED AND BOUND BY EDWARDS BROTHERS, INC.

The paper in this book meets the guidelines
for permanence and durability of the Committee
on Production Guidelines for Book Longevity
of the Council on Library Resources.

Library of Congress Cataloging-in-Publication Data

Finley, Lori, 1958–
        Traveling the Natchez Trace / by Lori Finley.
            p.   cm.
        Includes index.
        ISBN 0-89587-130-0: (alk. paper)
        1. Natchez Trace—Guidebooks.   I. Title.
    F217.N37F56   1995
    917.6—dc20   95-6023

To Dennis

Table of Contents

Preface

One of my earliest memories is of bouncing along in the backseat of my grandparents' car as a young girl. It was summer and we were driving through the flat farmlands of Mississippi under milky blue skies. Without a word, my grandfather pulled the car over to the side of the road and parked next to a field that seemed to stretch for miles. Ignoring my grandmother's questions, he opened his door, unfolded his long legs, and walked to the edge of the field. Peering out the window, I believed, as a self-absorbed five-year-old always believes, that whatever Gramps was doing had to be for me. And I was right. He returned to the car holding a long, reddish stalk of something that was foreign to my young eyes. Pulling his well-worn pocketknife from his trousers, he began peeling this strange-looking thing. Then, in his deep, booming voice, he called for my hand. And there he placed a classic Southern offering that I had never seen before: sugar cane.

Although I was born in Louisiana and spent a considerable part of my childhood in the Deep South, I now live in the shadow of the

Blue Ridge Mountains. So you can imagine what a pleasure it is to return to the part of the country where sugar-cane plantations, snow-white fields of cotton, and gracious Southern ways reign. It's like coming home again. I hope that you will join me on this step back into the Old South and one of its prettiest, most historic attractions: the Natchez Trace Parkway.

What exactly is the Natchez Trace Parkway?

The parkway is a paved two-lane road that runs from Nashville, Tennessee, to Natchez, Mississippi, with only three short uncompleted sections. The northern section at Nashville is scheduled to open in the spring of 1996. It is administered by the National Park Service and is similar in design to the Blue Ridge Parkway. Which means no commercial traffic. No development. No billboards. Though the parkway steers clear of large cities, many pleasant nearby towns offer travelers excellent lodging, restaurants, and other necessities.

This Southern landmark winds past rolling green farmland, past valleys filled with yellow wildflowers, and past majestic cypress trees rising from the still, black water of swamps. Don't be surprised to see white-tailed deer crossing the road. In fact, much of the parkway follows the original Natchez Trace, which began as a game trail. It subsequently served as an Indian trail. Much later, in the early eighteenth century, came the first white settlers. Over 180 separate sections of the original Trace are preserved within the parkway boundaries, so don't forget your hiking boots.

The Natchez Trace Parkway first came to my attention because of its popularity as a thin-tire bicycling route. As an avid cyclist, I am always interested in new regions to pedal. But as I explored, I discovered that there were as many attractions and highlights off the parkway as on it. The Trace is certainly ideal for touring on two wheels, but there are places worth seeing that are just a little too far to be reached by bicycle.

Though this guide is designed for car travel, don't restrict yourself to the sterile confines of your automobile. There are many opportunities to get out, stretch your legs, and prowl around.

Personally, I prefer to experience this land in its raw form, rather than through the filter of glass of my car window. How could I resist strolling along a path clothed by forests where Chickasaw Indians once quietly trod? Or roaming the site where Meriwether Lewis met his mysterious death? I will never forget the chilling sensation of looking down at the grave sites of unknown Confederate soldiers while distant thunder from a late-afternoon storm rumbled overhead, reminding me of the report of guns. And of course, I never would have had the experience had I stayed behind the wheel.

You can also expect a leisurely pace on the parkway. This is a part of the South that developed slowly and should, perhaps, be explored slowly. Even if you are a non-grits-eating Yankee accustomed to the fast pace of the North, you probably will find yourself shifting gears. To gain a true feeling of the rich heritage of this land, you will want to slow down. Smell the magnolias. Drink in the warm sunshine. And listen to the song of unseen crickets at dusk, that magical time between sunset and nightfall.

Acknowledgments

Researching this book was a wonderful experience for me. Rubbing elbows with some of the most fascinating people in Tennessee, Alabama, and Mississippi was a real privilege. Some of these folks are storehouses of facts and stories, which they are quick to tell to a willing listener. And I was willing. After sifting through their memories, they showered me with information. And in return, some wanted to know about me. Where was I from? Was I kin to any of the Finleys in southern Mississippi? How long ago did I live in Birmingham? They were as interested in climbing the branches of my family tree as I was in hearing their stories.

There are many people to whom I owe debts of gratitude for offering information or help with the research and writing of this book. First, my appreciation goes to the good folks at the Natchez Trace Parkway Headquarters in Tupelo. I wish to thank Jeff Penney, R. J. Callinan, and Marty Owens for providing quick answers to my questions. Don Thompson was also helpful in reviewing my manuscript and offering his advice.

I would hate to have to tally up the phone calls and visits that I made to chambers of commerce, visitor centers, museums, and other attractions during my research. Each person I spoke to at these sites was quick to mail or fax the information that I needed. I am grateful to them all, but I want to single out a few enthusiastic souls who really went out of their way to help. They are Liz Lovell in Columbia, Tennessee; Jimmie Cole in Tupelo, Mississippi; Margaret Rogers and Margaret Perkins in Corinth, Mississippi; Tricia Pace in Starkville, Mississippi; and Joanne Gordon and Ron Hill in Canton, Mississippi.

Others who helped me in various stages of this project were Terence J. Winschel, Bob Dodson, Stacy Allen, Dale Smith, Jim Atkinson, Betty Searcy, Angie Costner, Roy Costner, Midge Luttrell, Robbie Cox, and Lamar Williams.

I especially want to thank Kay Jones of the Natchez Trace Bed-and-Breakfast Reservation Service for extensive information on both lodgings and restaurants. Following her tips, I had several delightful conversations with charming Southern innkeepers and restaurateurs.

As always, the staff of John F. Blair, Publisher, was a tremendous team in the production of this book. My thanks go to Judy Breakstone, Sue Clark, Margaret Couch, Debbie Hampton, Liza Langrall, Carolyn Sakowski, Anne Schultz, Heath Simpson, Lisa Wagoner, and Andrew Waters. I particularly want to express my heart-felt thanks to Steve Kirk, who was especially thoughtful and industrious during the editorial process. His suggestions greatly improved this book.

My friend and compatriot, Dennis Coello, deserves a special thank-you. In addition to supplying many of the photographs in this book, he helped me immensely during the initial stages of writing. While sipping coffee on the opposite end of a telephone line, Dennis was always willing to give me advice.

And finally, thanks go to my wonderful family—Bob, Erin, and Elizabeth—for surviving yet another deadline. They were good sports even when my hectic schedule resulted in towering piles of neglected laundry and soup-and-sandwich suppers, on a *good* night! Bob's love and steady encouragement were my mainstays. However, my greatest reward is seeing the pride in my sweet daughters' faces as they show off books written by their "author mom."

Introduction

For those weary of congested interstate highways and the blur of faces on crowded city streets, the Natchez Trace Parkway is a haven. Clear blue skies, paper-white blossoms of dogwood trees, the smell of freshly mown grass, and bird song are sure to appeal to those looking for a relaxing change of pace.

Though the natural surroundings are some of the most alluring in the country, there's much more to the Natchez Trace. Rich in attractions, the parkway and its surrounding towns can occupy visitors for weeks. But don't expect to find yourself queuing up in line for the Tilt-A-Whirl. Such attractions are, thankfully, nowhere to be found on the Natchez Trace Parkway.

What you will find are dozens of historic sites, impressive military battlefields, and Indian burial grounds. There are also murky swamps where alligators lurk, shadowy trails to hike, and places rumored to be the eerie dancing grounds of witches.

And then, of course, there are the enchanting antebellum homes that call up thoughts of Tara and Scarlett O'Hara. Homes like these spring to mind when we think of the Old South. Picture yourself driving down a plantation avenue canopied by the graceful limbs of live oak trees. Imagine for a moment stepping onto a white-columned porch and sitting down in an antique wicker rocker that creaks with your every move.

Think of the sounds such antebellum walls might remember. Maybe the rustle of petticoats hiding beneath a Southern belle's gown. Or the sound of a crisply starched, white damask tablecloth being snapped open and draped over a mahogany dining table. Perhaps the clink of a demitasse cup meeting its saucer or even the clatter of a sterling silver spoon dropped onto a gleaming hardwood floor.

These remnants of a bygone age embody the spirit of the Old South. They are reminders of a cultural and social history unlike any other in America. As you tour this area, you may be struck with a feeling of timelessness. You may also come to believe that the days of mint-julep afternoons and Southern gentility have not been lost altogether.

Closely following the original Natchez Trace, the parkway leads contemporary travelers beside one of the most historic routes in America. The Trace has a storied past that stretches as far back as perhaps the early 1600s. Winding from Tennessee's Cumberland River Valley across the southwestern corner of Alabama and finally threading through Mississippi to its final destination in Natchez, this old footpath had humble beginnings.

The Trace was carved into being by the paws and hooves of wild animals and the moccasin-clad feet of Chickasaw and Choctaw Indians. Later came French explorers, pioneers, frontiersmen, post riders, itinerant preachers, and soldiers. Travelers from all walks of life followed this early frontier road. Andrew Jackson, later the seventh president of the United States, was a frequent traveler. Meriwether Lewis of the famed Lewis and Clark expedition also passed this way. Lewis died under mysterious circumstances at an inn here, giving the Trace a melancholy touch of fame. John James Audubon was no stranger to the Trace; he spent many days along its southern stretches painting birds.

Considered the most vital overland route between the early settlements of Natchez and Nashville, the Trace saw its heyday during a forty-year period that began with the arrival of boatmen in the late 1700s. These men built flatboats and barges, loaded them with goods from places as far away as Pennsylvania, Virginia, and Kentucky, and floated down the Mississippi River. It was Natchez or bust. Upon arrival, they broke up the barges and sold the goods they had floated down the river—tobacco, iron, rope, flour—as well as the lumber from the flatboats. Why did they destroy perfectly good boats? By the time they reached Natchez, the barges were of no use to them. The only way to return home was to either row against the strong currents of the Mississippi or hoof it up the Trace. The latter was the obvious choice.

The local folk around Natchez referred to the boatmen as "Kaintucks," probably because most of them hailed from Kentucky. They were a rough and rowdy bunch and apparently had an appearance to match. Alexander Wilson, renowned artist and ornithologist and close friend of Meriwether Lewis, described them as being "dirty as Hottentots, their dress a shirt and trousers of canvass, black, greasy, and sometimes in tatters, the skin burnt wherever exposed to the sun, each with a budget [a small bag or pouch], wrapt up in an old blanket, their beards eighteen days old, added to the singularity of their appearance, which was altogether savage."

During the period of the Kaintucks, the Trace grew from a narrow wilderness trail to a wide, heavily trampled frontier road. But when the whistles of the first steamboats began filling the air over the tea-colored waters of the Mississippi, the days of the Natchez Trace were numbered. It wasn't long before the boatmen began boarding the steamboats for a much more comfortable return trip home. And it was then that the Trace met its demise.

Though the tales of the past have a romantic ring to them, the early days of the Natchez Trace were extremely difficult and dangerous. The tangled forests were breeding grounds for thieves lurking in the brush. And understandably, the Indians did not greet the white settlers with glasses of ice-cold lemonade and slices of pecan pie.

Even when pioneer travelers weren't in jeopardy of having their loads lightened by robbers or of having Indians threaten them with a new haircut, they had other dangers to face. There were poisonous snakes. Floods. Lightning storms. Killer tornadoes.

The discomforts of travel were great as well. When heavy rains turned the Trace into a path of deep mud, progress became unbelievably slow or downright impossible. Imagine trying to coax a team of oxen into pulling out a wagon mired in mud, all the while watching for rattlesnakes and slapping mosquitoes feasting on your exposed skin. Sounds like a fun trip, doesn't it?

An exhibit along the Natchez Trace Parkway chronicles travel in those early days. Part of it reads, "This early interstate road building venture produced a snake-infested, mosquito-beset, robber-haunted, Indian-pestered forest path. Lamented by the pious, cussed by the impious, it tried everyone's strength and patience."

The Trace also saw the tragic clash of war. The blood of thousands of Confederate and Union soldiers was spilled on and around this frontier path. Today, monuments honoring the dead can be found almost anywhere you look. They range from simple gravestones to elaborate military parks like that in Vicksburg. If you have the opportunity to talk to local folk about the Civil War, you will notice that they simply refer to it as "the War," just as the mighty Mississippi River is referred to, simply, as "the River."

Though most talk of the Civil War is somber, there are a few lighthearted stories. One story questions the loyalties of some of the ladies left behind by their soldier husbands. It seems that while many towns were burned almost completely to the ground by torch-wielding Yankees, a few were spared. Union strategy? Perhaps. But many, with slightly raised eyebrows, suggest that credit is due a few Southern women for saving many of the antebellum sites. It is speculated that these beautiful belles kept the Union troops so pleasantly preoccupied that they forgot all about burning down the plantation homes. I suppose that the old saying must be true: All's fair in love and war.

The beauty of the Natchez Trace Parkway is that it offers something to almost everyone. Few places so accessible offer such a varied, pretty trip off the beaten path. Whether you're interested in a weekend getaway, a Sunday drive, a two-week vacation, a camping trip, or a bicycling expedition, the parkway and its surrounding towns are bound to meet your needs.

Beginning southwest of Nashville on TN 96, the parkway ends 450 miles later a few miles north of Natchez, Mississippi, on U.S. 61. There are three short uncompleted sections: the northern terminus, the southern terminus, and a section in Jackson, Mississippi. Before traveling, check with the parkway headquarters to determine if these sections have been completed. Milepost markers on the eastern side of the Trace count down the miles to Natchez. The speed limit is an *enforced* fifty miles per hour. Those of you with a lead foot had better watch it or you might get the added bonus of touring city hall.

This travel guide should in no way be considered a comprehensive listing of all the highlights found on or near the Natchez Trace Parkway. Obviously, an all-inclusive description of the attractions in every city and town along the Trace could not possibly be confined to a single book. The sites that I chose to include are some of the most popular in the area, some that I particularly enjoyed, and some that were recommended to me by good sources. They vary from places where historical incidents occurred to sites that give visitors a true taste of the Old South.

Some of the highlights have an obvious connection to the Natchez Trace, such as the Hermitage in Nashville. This popular tourist attraction was the home of Andrew Jackson, a frequent traveler on the old footpath. Others, such as Belle Meade Plantation, were included for their historical significance, as well as their proximity to the Trace. I have also included a few sites, such as the Olde Country Bakery in Brooksville, Mississippi, simply because of their popularity. When local folk tell me I *must* visit a certain attraction before leaving the area, I usually heed the advice.

Travelers on the Natchez Trace will see remnants of Indian days, such as the odd mounds that dot the parkway. There are also natural highlights, such as waterfalls, swamps, and caves. Some of these attractions may not interest you, or you may discover other appealing spots I have not mentioned.

Allow your personality to dictate your choices. If you would be bored to tears spending more than thirty seconds learning about the mining of iron ore, then skip that attraction. Or if you're the kind of person who could drive up the winding dirt road to the romantic ruins of Windsor Plantation only to find yourself muttering, "What's the big deal?" then you're better off ignoring that side trip.

When planning your trip, bear in mind that the busiest travel times on the Natchez Trace Parkway are during June, July, and August. Expect crowds and a good bit of traffic, especially along the popular southern stretches and on weekends. And remember that Dixie is hot, sultry, and sticky in the summer. Come armed with bug repellant, an air conditioner, and a good attitude.

Autumn brings cooler temperatures and that long-awaited chill to bare arms. It also brings skies so stunningly blue that you may wince. Though the skies are beautiful, the changing colors of the leaves steal the show. Glowing reds, oranges, and yellows seem to set the forest on fire. This celebration of color is fairly late; don't expect to see the leaves at their peak until the last weeks of October. Fortunately, the state of Tennessee offers a seasonal prerecorded message called the Fall Color Hotline, which provides information on fall foliage.

Winter is often a pleasant time of year to travel the Trace, partly because of the mild temperature. Once in a blue moon, the area gets a light dusting of snow, but it rarely outlives more than a few sparkling morning hours. Also, traffic is virtually nonexistent, mosquitoes are but a distant memory, and plantation homes and other attractions are almost crowd-free.

During the holidays, many of the old towns along the Trace look like Currier and Ives prints, sans the snow. Dressed in garlands of greenery and glittering white lights, the old Southern homes become even more beautiful in their holiday finery. Night comes early this time of year, taking December days by surprise. On a late-afternoon drive, the yellow glow streaming from windows draped with pungent evergreen boughs and bright red ribbons is a warm, inviting sight.

But without a doubt, spring is the season of splendor on the Natchez Trace Parkway. Eyes weary of winter's dull gray landscape will glory in the sight of creamy magnolia blossoms, delicate dogwood flowers, yellow daffodils, and red azaleas. Buds begin sprouting on trees. Days become warmer and longer as the season unfolds. And finally, as the hardwoods leaf out, species by species and day by day, the forests seem to explode into one thousand shades of green.

For ease of travel, I have divided the Trace into thirteen chapters, each of which constitutes a half-day or full-day tour. I urge you, however, not to mistake each chapter for a travel agent's itinerary. This guide is written to provide recommendations for getting the most out of the Trace, but that does not mean you must do it all. Pick and choose. You may want to combine several chapters for a single day's tour, or you may be so intrigued with one spot that you decide to linger there for an entire weekend.

Also, don't let the long list of attractions in each chapter rush you. In the past, I have made the mistake of traveling with people who had schedules written in stone. As travel companions go, they should have been shot and tossed to the buzzards the first day. Keeping an anxious eye on the clock and feeling rushed because there are still more stops on the day's travel plan can ruin a vacation.

Each chapter begins with a summary of the length and endpoints of the tour. The total mileage of each tour includes the distance to and from sites off the parkway, if any. Next comes a milepost guide, which references points of interest and services, giving you quick, at-a-glance information on the tour. If you are wondering where you can find picnic tables for spreading out the contents of a lunch hamper or how to locate a rest room for that child in the backseat threatening to burst, then turn to this section.

The milepost guide is followed by an in-depth discussion of the attractions you will encounter.

At the end of the chapter comes a summary of nearby services. Though there are campgrounds in many places, inexpensive chain motels in nearby towns, and bed-and-breakfast inns galore, I purposely avoided listing each and every one. The addresses and telephone numbers of each town's chamber of commerce are listed in the appendix; check with the appropriate agency for more comprehensive lodging information. However, for each chapter, I have provided information on parkway-managed campgrounds, bed-and-breakfast inns offered by the Natchez Trace Bed-and-Breakfast Reservation Service, and other unique lodgings.

I also recommend restaurants on the route of each tour. Most of those mentioned are establishments where I enjoyed an especially good Southern meal, such as a plate of savory fried catfish and hushpuppies or a table heaped high with a mound of boiled, bright red, peel-and-eat crawfish. Though I didn't have a meal at every one of the places listed, I chose to include them because they came highly recommended by local folk. The restaurants listed represent but a tiny percentage of the excellent eating establishments found near the Natchez Trace Parkway. This is a region where the cuisine is unparalleled, in my opinion. A listing of all the nook-and-cranny gumbo shops, coffee houses serving New Orleans–style beignets and café au lait, and fine Southern restaurants would alone constitute an entire book.

Each tour also includes a general map. However, I strongly recommend that you supplement this book's maps with the National Park Service's *Official Map and Guide of the Natchez Trace Parkway*. This is an excellent resource to have at your side while traveling the Trace. You can write or call the parkway headquarters to obtain this free foldout map.

For easy reference, an appendix is included at the back of the book. It contains the addresses and telephone numbers of museums, parks, historic homes, chambers of commerce, etc. If you need more information after reading about a particular tour, chances are good that the appendix will refer you to the proper agency.

The Natchez Trace Parkway opens the door to the past. It also opens the door to the adventure of exploration. Whether you are a true-blue Southerner who can say the name of William Tecumseh Sherman only through clenched teeth or a Northerner whose deprived taste buds have never known a spoonful of buttered grits, you are bound to be captured by the intriguing spell of the Trace. So buckle up. It's time to go. South that is, to the Natchez Trace Parkway.

TRAVELING THE
NATCHEZ TRACE

N

TENNESSEE

The Hermitage
TN 45
To Lebanon

65
40

NASHVILLE

65

● Belle Meade

Old Hickory Blvd.
TN 100
40

● Pasquo
Proposed
Future Terminus ●
Franklin ●
TN 96

440
TN 96
Linton ●
Temporary Terminus
430
TN 16
● Leipers Fork
65

● Garrison Creek

TN 46
● Old Trace

● Burns Branch
● Spring Hill

● Tennessee Valley Divide

420
31

TN 100

● Water Valley Overlook
410
Columbia
Shady Grove ●
TN 50

● ● ● ● ● Tour
▬▬▬▬▬ Natchez Trace Parkway

BELLE MEADE PLANTATION

NASHVILLE TO WATER VALLEY OVERLOOK

TOTAL MILEAGE
*Approximately 60 miles
(Mileage varies with starting
point.)*
TOUR ENDPOINTS
*This tour begins in Nashville,
Tennessee, and ends near
Milepost 408 on the parkway.*

Milepost Guide

450.0   FUTURE TERMINUS

The National Park Service plans to open this terminus in early 1996.

437.6   TEMPORARY TERMINUS

At the time of this writing, the Natchez Trace Parkway ended at TN 96 south of Nashville. Tupelo, Mississippi, the location of the parkway headquarters, is 179 miles south of this milepost.

428.2   HIGHWAY INTERSECTION

TN 46 crosses the Natchez Trace Parkway here. Exit the

parkway to reach the village of Leipers Fork, located east of the parkway. There is a public telephone at Leipers Fork Grocery.

427.5   GARRISON CREEK
This site offers rest rooms, picnic tables (some sheltered), and a 24.5-mile trail for hikers and equestrians which extends from the parking area to S.R. 50 at Duck River, Milepost 408. A large, paved parking area and hitches for tethering horses are provided. For information on organized horseback rides, see the appendix.

426.2   OLD TRACE
This section of the Old Trace offers an easy twenty-minute hike.

425.2   BURNS BRANCH
Located on the east side of the parkway, this site offers picnic tables and access to the Garrison Creek trail.

423.9   TENNESSEE VALLEY DIVIDE
A parking area is located on the east side of the parkway here.

418.2   HIGHWAY INTERSECTION
TN 7 intersects the parkway here.

411.8   WATER VALLEY OVERLOOK
This site offers picnic tables and a scenic valley view.

407.9   HIGHWAY INTERSECTION
TN 50 crosses the parkway here. Columbia, Tennessee, is located approximately fifteen miles east on TN 50.

The northern terminus of the Natchez Trace Parkway lies a few miles south of Tennessee's "Music City, USA," otherwise known as Nashville. Nashville is the largest city on the Trace, and its long list of attractions may tempt you to stay awhile before beginning your tour of the parkway.

Since Nashville is known worldwide as the home of country music, it's no surprise that the vast majority of its attractions have a musical bent. Everywhere you turn, music can be found. You can take in the sights and, of course, the sounds of the incredible Grand Ole Opry; Barbara Mandrell Country; Music Village, USA; and Opryland. There is also the Hank Williams, Jr., Museum; the Country Music Hall of Fame; the Willie Nelson and Friends Showcase Museum; the House of Cash; and the Music Valley Wax Museum, to name but a few.

Country music has taken Nashville by storm. Producing hit songs with lyrics like "Bubba shot the jukebox 'coz he didn't like the song" has become big business in this city. You can find recording studios of almost every country label in Nashville. But don't look for shiny, towering recording complexes housing deal-making fat cats. For the most part, the studios along Music Row are quite modest. Even Sony, king of the country music industry, is housed in unpretentious surroundings.

Many of these companies have converted antebellum homes into recording offices. Million-dollar deals are struck and huge hits are born in old Southern houses with slowly turning ceiling fans, creaking wooden floors, and windows dressed with fluttering lace curtains.

The city has come a long way from its beginnings. Fort Nashborough was established long after the city of Natchez, located at the southern end of the Natchez Trace Parkway, was settled by white men. In fact, the area that is now Nashville was unsettled as late as 1779. This vast wilderness was inhabited only by Indians and a few daring French hunters and traders. Considered a hunting paradise because of the abundant game attracted to the region's salt-bearing rocks, the area became known as "French Lick" or "Big Salt Lick."

Word of the promising hunting and trapping here soon leaked over the green hills and into surrounding states. In the late 1700s, a group of would-be settlers was formed by a North Carolinian named Richard Henderson. Henderson appointed Englishman James Robertson—who later became known as the "Father of Tennessee"—and Colonel John Donelson leaders of the expedition. Robertson led a group of men and livestock overland, while Donelson led the older men, the women, and the children on a flotilla of boats down the Tennessee, Ohio, and Cumberland rivers. Donelson's daughter

Rachel, who later became Andrew Jackson's bride, was among those in the river group. The rest of his family also accompanied him on what became an extremely hazardous journey.

The overland and river parties left separately from Fort Patrick Henry in North Carolina's newly established Watauga settlement in late 1779.

Despite bitter temperatures and numerous hardships, Robertson's party arrived at the site of present-day Nashville and crossed the icy Cumberland River on Christmas Day 1779. The men built a stockade and crude cabins along the bluffs of the river and named the site Fort Nashborough, in honor of Revolutionary War hero General Francis Nash.

Donelson's group arrived in the spring of 1780 after an extremely grueling journey. The harsh winter weather brought difficult problems, including illness. Some members of the river party came down with smallpox and fell behind the rest of the group. Indians took advantage of their weakened state and ambushed the settlers, killing many of them.

The members of Robertson's party waiting at Fort Nashborough were jubilant when Donelson's party was spotted coming down the river.

In a final entry in his diary, Donelson wrote, "This day we arrived at our journey's end at the Big Salt Lick, where we have the pleasure of finding Captain Robertson and his company. It is a source of satisfaction to us to be enabled to restore to him and others their families and friends who were entrusted to our care and who sometimes sensed, perhaps, despair of ever meeting again."

If you are approaching Nashville from the east on Interstate 40, you may want to visit the Hermitage, which is the former home of Andrew Jackson, the seventh president of the United States and a man closely linked to the Natchez Trace for many years. To reach it, exit onto TN 45 (Andrew Jackson Parkway) at the sign for the Hermitage. Drive 3.1 miles to the turnoff for the Hermitage, which is on the right.

This National Historic Landmark is one of Nashville's most popular attractions. In addition to the mansion, there is a gift shop, a museum, and a theater, where a sixteen-minute interpretational film is shown. Guides will provide you with cassette players offering audio tours of the estate.

THE HERMITAGE

Inside the mansion are original antique furnishings, imported wallpaper, and musical instruments which belonged to the Jackson family. You will also see the former president's bedroom and his beautiful four-poster mahogany bed. This is where Old Hickory drew his last breath. At his side were his adopted son, Andrew, and Andrew's wife, Sarah. Be sure to notice the two windows that overlook the porch. It was through these windows that Jackson's many servants tearfully watched during his last hours of life.

Outside are the kitchen, the smokehouse, a formal garden, and original log cabins. Located in the family cemetery is Jackson's tomb, where the former president and his beloved wife, Rachel, lie in state.

There are several ways to access the Natchez Trace Parkway from the Nashville area.

The most direct route to the future northern terminus from Interstate 40 is by taking Exit 192 and driving south on McCrory Lane for four miles toward Pasquo. From the stop sign at the intersection with TN 100, the parkway will be visible on the right. The Loveless Cafe and Motel is on the left.

To reach the current terminus of the Natchez Trace Parkway, turn south off Interstate 40 onto Interstate 65. Take Exit 65 off Interstate

65 and drive west on TN 96 for approximately 2.5 miles to downtown Franklin. This quaint town is filled with historic homes and other attractions. Chances are that you will not want to blast straight through without stopping.

"Fifteen miles and 100 years down the road from Nashville, Franklin is the place to shop and dine in historic elegance," reads a Downtown Franklin Association promotion. And it's true. The entire fifteen-block original downtown area, including the quaint shopping district on Main Street, is listed on the National Register of Historic Places. Renovated and restored buildings dating to the 1800s house about fifty specialty shops, including art galleries, boutiques, and restaurants. Hailed as "the Antique Capital of Tennessee," Franklin is brimming with antique shops and auction houses. Walking tours are offered in the town. Four festivals are held here annually.

Franklin also has its share of ghosts. As in so many Southern cities, many of the antebellum homes come complete with chain-clanking, howling "haints." Quite a few families even refer to their resident ghouls by name.

The Bennett House is no exception. To reach this home from TN 96, turn onto Main Street and drive west of the downtown square. Turn right onto Fourth Avenue North; the Bennett House is on the right.

This house was built in the 1870s by Walter James Bennett, who served in the Confederate army. When he returned from the war, he went into the hardware business with his father. The Bennett name was known for over one hundred years in Franklin's business circles. In fact, the hardware store was a favorite meeting place for town residents.

Today, the Bennett House is a private recording studio. It is frequently used as a lodging by artists from out of town. Quite often, these musical guests have had hair-raising brushes with the ghost of the Bennett House.

Randall Griffith, keyboard player in the group Dixiana, recalls a time when he stayed overnight at the Bennett House. During the wee hours of the night, he was abruptly awakened by a startling sound. Thinking that someone had dropped a metal trash can from the second floor onto the first floor, he bolted out of bed to investigate. In fact, everyone in the house got up to see what was going on. They were soon ushered back to their rooms by the resident recording engineer, who was accustomed to the midnight awakenings. "Y'all

PART OF THE CARTER HOUSE ESTATE

just go back to bed," the engineer drawled, "it's only Walter the ghost." Though the house remained quiet for the remainder of the night, lights mysteriously turned off and on. Randall says he never did fall back asleep.

From the Bennett House, return to the downtown square and turn right onto TN 96. Drive one block to Church Street and turn right. After 0.25 mile, turn left onto Columbia Avenue. Drive 0.3 mile to West Fowlkes Street and turn right. The Carter House is on the left.

This historic house was built in the 1830s by F. B. Carter. It was caught in the Battle of Franklin, one of the bloodiest battles of the Civil War, during which twelve Confederate generals, more than two thousand Union soldiers, and more than six thousand Confederate soldiers lost their lives. Tod Carter, a Confederate lieutenant, was mortally wounded in battle. He was taken to this home, where his family huddled fearfully in the basement. Carter died two days later.

Today, visitors to the battle-scarred house can still see the holes made by bullets that ripped into the bricks. The Carter House and several other original buildings from Mr. Carter's farm are considered the most heavily damaged buildings still standing from the Civil War.

A video presentation on the Battle of Franklin is offered at the visitor center. A museum is also located here. Guided tours of the

Nashville to Water Valley Overlook

house and grounds are offered daily. A living-history program is acted out annually in November, giving visitors an idea of what daily life was like during the dark days of the Civil War.

If you have time for one more stop before leaving the Franklin area, plan to see Carnton Plantation. From the Carter House, return to Columbia Avenue and turn right. Drive 0.2 mile and turn left at the stoplight onto Cleburne Street. Drive 0.3 mile to Lewisburg Avenue and turn right. Drive an additional 0.3 mile to Carnton Lane. Turn right and follow the signs to the plantation.

Another survivor of the Civil War, Carnton Plantation was built in 1826 by Randal McGavock. It served as a field hospital during the Battle of Franklin. Hundreds of soldiers died under the roof of this elegant country estate. During the night of the battle, the bodies of four Confederate generals were brought to the plantation and placed on the two-story veranda that swept across the back of the house.

Two years after the battle, two acres adjacent to the family cemetery were designated for the burial of more than one thousand young men from the South who lost their lives in the Battle of Franklin. Today, the cemetery is considered the largest private Confederate burial site in America.

BELLE MEADE PLANTATION

Before the war, Carnton Plantation knew happier times. Randal McGavock was a former mayor of Nashville, and his stately home was the site of frequent political and social gatherings. Visitors included Sam Houston and the seventh and eleventh presidents of the United States, Andrew Jackson and James K. Polk.

Now that your touring legs are warmed up, it's time to head to the Natchez Trace Parkway. From Carnton Plantation, retrace your path to the Carter House, downtown Franklin, and TN 96. Drive west on TN 96 for 8.4 miles. Turn left at the sign for the parkway. After 0.5 mile, you will reach a stop sign at the parkway itself. Turn left. At the time of this writing, this point served as the temporary northern terminus of the parkway. The National Park Service plans to extend the parkway to its final northern terminus at TN 100, leading directly into Nashville.

If you are approaching Nashville from the west on Interstate 40, you may want to stop at Belle Meade Plantation. Take Exit 204, where you will see a sign for Belle Meade. Drive south on TN 155 (Robertson Road) for 2.3 miles. Turn right onto U.S. 70 South (Harding Road) and drive 1.6 miles. Turn left at the sign for Belle Meade. You will actually see the mansion on the left and pass it before reaching the turnoff.

Nashville's pre-Civil War belles are long gone. Their days of dancing all night with Southern gentlemen and being courted by beaus under wisteria-draped oaks on moonlit evenings are now only memories. But one belle is still around. She is Nashville's Belle Meade Plantation, also known as "the Queen of Tennessee Plantations."

Belle Meade began modestly in 1790 as a log cabin inn on the Natchez Trace. During its early years, this prominent plantation, tucked away in the rolling green hills of Tennessee, was the center of high society. Later, it became world-renowned as a thorough-bred stable. It was home to Iroquois, the first and only American-bred winner of the English Derby.

Built in 1853, the Greek Revival mansion is the focal point of the plantation. Quite a few famous guests spent the night at Belle Meade, including President Grover Cleveland and his wife. Later, in the early 1900s, President William Howard Taft sent word that he would be visiting Belle Meade. Since Taft, at three-hundred-plus pounds, was no small man, the news sent the staff scurrying to work. They worried that the guest baths were too small to accommodate the president's girth. Ultimately, one of the upstairs baths had to be completely remodeled prior to his visit.

Today, visitors to Belle Meade can tour the mansion and see the original furnishings. The original log cabin still stands, somehow miraculously spared by the torch-wielding Yankees during the Civil War. In fact, the log cabin is touted as one of the oldest houses in Tennessee. There is also a carriage house, a stable, a smokehouse, and a dairy house. Costumed guides are available to answer any questions you have.

To reach the future terminus of the Natchez Trace Parkway from Belle Meade, visitors will turn left onto U.S. 70 South when they exit the property, then drive west for 0.6 mile to the intersection with TN 100, then bear left on TN 100 and drive 7.5 miles to the intersection with the parkway.

To reach the current northern terminus from Belle Meade, return to Interstate 40 and drive east to Interstate 65. Head south on Interstate 65 to Franklin. Follow the directions detailed earlier to access the parkway from Franklin.

As soon as you turn off the busy Tennessee highways and onto the parkway, things change dramatically. The speed limit drops to fifty miles per hour, slowing down both your vehicle and your mood. From TN 96 southward to TN 46, for approximately ten miles, the speed limit is forty miles per hour. The scenery seems to slow down as well. Gone is the bustle of Nashville. Traffic congestion, neon lights, and billboards are replaced by dogwood trees, rustic split-rail fences, and grassy road shoulders strewn with wildflowers.

The first stop is Garrison Creek, located on the east side of the parkway south of Milepost 428. Named for a garrison of army troops stationed here in the early 1800s, this site now serves as both a picnic area and a trailhead for equestrians and hikers. Some picnic tables are situated beneath the wooden park-service shelter, while others are canopied by tree limbs. The cool shade of either creates a pleasant setting for a midday picnic. A 24.5-mile trail begins behind the shelter and extends all the way to S.R. 50 at Duck River, near Milepost 408.

Near Milepost 426 is a section of the Old Trace cleared by the

TYPICAL SCENE ON THE PARKWAY

Dennis Coello

Nashville to Water Valley Overlook

United States Army in 1801. This historic wilderness road connected Nashville, on the Cumberland River, with Natchez, on the Mississippi River. It was known in earlier days as the Natchez Road. This section of the original Trace will give you a good opportunity to stretch your legs on a short stroll back in time. As you walk this section, you may find yourself calling up images of the weary travelers who trudged mile after mile of this path so many years ago.

The next stop along the parkway is the Tennessee Valley Divide, near Milepost 424. This long, high ridge dividing central Tennessee reaches elevations of 1,100 feet, the highest along the entire length of the Natchez Trace. Streams south of the divide flow into the Duck and Tennessee rivers, while streams north flow into the Cumberland River. While this information may have you wondering if a pop quiz is imminent, these facts were critically important to early travelers along the Trace. Though the rise and fall of the divide is almost imperceptible in an automobile, the slightest changes in elevation made a huge difference to those on horseback and on foot.

The divide was also important to early travelers because it marked the boundary between Chickasaw Indian land and the state of Tennessee. When hunters and trappers reached the divide on their northward expeditions, they could finally relax. Nashville was now only a stone's throw away and, more important, they had reached the end of Indian territory.

This chapter's tour of the parkway ends here. If you wish to visit the town of Columbia, exit the parkway onto TN 50 near Milepost 408. Drive east for 12.8 miles to a stop sign; turn left to continue on TN 50. Drive an additional 1.1 miles to a stoplight; continue straight through this intersection. You are now on U.S. 412, which becomes West Seventh Street in Columbia. Follow West Seventh for 1.7 miles to Columbia's downtown square. A description of Columbia and its accommodations and restaurants is included in the next chapter.

Bed-and-Breakfast Inns

ASHLAND CITY

Birdsong Country Inn
1306 TN 49 East
Ashland City, TN 37015
(800) 377-2770 or (615) 285-2777

This cedar-log lodge, built in 1910, is located a pleasant twenty-minute drive from Nashville at Milepost 450 of the parkway, a section currently under construction. Built by the Cheek family of Maxwell House Coffee fame, it is listed on the National Register of Historic Places. The inn boasts an extensive collection of art and antiques, a great room with a massive stone fireplace, a screened porch, and a heated Jacuzzi on the patio. The guest rooms are spacious. If you arrive early in the afternoon and don't plan to tour the Natchez Trace until the following day, you may want to take a stroll along a nearby creek. Or you may want to grab a good book and just relax in a hammock strung between stately trees outside the lodge. In the morning, a gourmet continental breakfast is served with coffee that is, of course, good to the last drop.

FRANKLIN

Lyric Springs Country Inn
7306 South Harpeth Road
Franklin, TN 37064
(615) 799-9613 or (800) 621-7824

Featured in *Country Inn* and *Better Homes and Gardens* magazines, this inn has a decidedly country feel to it. The tables are covered with quilts and needlework. Other homespun articles decorate the guest rooms. Located close to Nashville, the inn obviously has caught the country music bug, its lounge decorated with memorabilia of the stars. Don your cowboy hat and bring your horse, pardner. Nearby trails may be used by equestrians; stables are available for overnight boarding.

Magnolia House Bed-and-Breakfast

1317 Columbia Avenue
Franklin, TN 37064
(615) 794-8178

This two-story cottage is located a block and a half south of the Carter House and within walking distance of the historic downtown area. It offers three air-conditioned rooms and private baths.

LEIPERS FORK

Namaste Barn Bed-and-Breakfast

5436 Leipers Creek Road
Franklin, TN 37064
(800) 377-2770 or (615) 285-2777

This country home is located just minutes from Milepost 436 off the Natchez Trace Parkway. It sits in the quaint Leipers Creek Valley near the village of Leipers Fork. It features large guest rooms with private baths, a swimming pool, and an exercise room. A full breakfast is offered in the mornings.

DUCK RIVER

McEwen Farm Log Cabin

P.O. Box 97
Duck River, TN 38454
(615) 583-2378

To reach this bed-and-breakfast inn, take TN 50 West at

Milepost 407.9 on the parkway and drive toward Centerville for 2.1 miles. Turn right onto Bratton Lane. The inn is located on the right after 0.5 mile.

Unique Dining

NASHVILLE

Loveless Cafe
Route 5, Highway 100
Nashville, TN 37221
(615) 646-9700

This quaint restaurant is located 0.1 mile east of the future northern terminus of the parkway at Milepost 450. Featured on "CBS This Morning" as one of the five best places in America for breakfast, it hosts celebrities and local folk alike. Martha Stewart is quoted as saying of her meal here, "It was the best breakfast I've ever had." Jefferson Morgan of *Bon Appetit* said, "On a scale of 1 to 10, my breakfast came in at about a 14."

So what's all the fuss about? For starters, it's the delicious country ham and red-eye gravy. Loveless also keeps its tables filled with "scratch" biscuits, served piping hot with thick slabs of butter and homemade peach and blackberry preserves. Bottles of sorghum molasses adorn each table.

Despite the national acclaim, this down-home restaurant seems unfazed by fame. Guests are seated in an unpretentious setting of scuffed wooden floors, wood-paneled walls, bright red curtains, and slowly turning ceiling fans. The place doesn't seem to have changed a bit in the thirty-five years it has been in business. Well-worn hinges on the swinging kitchen door are kept busy as plate-laden waitresses burst from the kitchen, trailed by the clatter of kitchen sounds.

Loveless also serves lunch and dinner; the Southern fried chicken is outstanding. Both tourists and locals make a beeline for the vittles here, so you would be wise to make reservations before you go.

FRANKLIN

Choices Restaurant

Main Street and Fourth Avenue
Franklin, TN 37064
(615) 791-0001

Guests are enveloped by beautiful surroundings as soon as they walk into this restaurant, located in historic downtown Franklin. High ceilings, glowing candles, and windows adorned with lace panels give diners a feel of the Old South. Lunch and dinner are served in true Southern style.

Merridee's Bread Basket

110 Fourth Avenue South
Franklin, TN 37064
(615) 790-3755

Blue-and-white gingham tablecloths, wooden floors, and baskets hanging from the ceiling welcome you the moment you step into Merridee's. The delicious smells of freshly brewed coffee, home-made bread baking in huge ovens, and cinnamon wafting through the air are sure to whet your appetite for breakfast. Sandwiches, salads, and homemade soups are the fare for lunch, with box lunches available if you plan to picnic along the Natchez Trace Parkway. Merridee's is closed for dinner.

LEIPERS FORK

Ernie's Smokehouse

3302 Bailey Road
Leipers Fork, TN 37064
(615) 790-0117

Ernie and Doneda Woodard run this restaurant, which features delicious barbecue. Ernie crafted his own smoker, which he uses to cook ribs, chicken, and hams. Meanwhile, Doneda bakes "cornlight" bread—a sweeter version of classic cornbread—and all the desserts.

The restaurant is housed in the former Green's Grocery Store, built in 1914. The Woodards stumbled upon a real treasure while they were restoring the building. It seems that the former proprietor of the store, Herman Green, had scrawled "important" dates on an old almanac calendar and the surrounding wall. Many of the dates go back decades. His notations show when he planted tomatoes and beans in his garden, when he got a haircut, and when he had his truck repaired. Doneda laughingly told me that they even found a note from 1961 revealing when he "put the cow to the bull."

Ernie and Doneda couldn't bring themselves to paint over Mr. Green's colorful chronology of his years, so the calendar and wall have been left intact. If you stop by Ernie's, you will see them in a corner under the original Green's Grocery Store sign.

Try to visit Ernie's on a Tuesday night, because that is "Songwriter Night." Musicians come from far and wide to pick and sing. Not surprisingly, the crowd is standing room only. The restaurant also features live music on weekend nights.

Duck River

Duck River

410 ● Water Valley
Overlook

Duck River

Columbia

Shady Grove ●

TN
50

Gordon House and Ferry Site

Baker Bluff
Overlook ●

Rattle and Snap
Plantation ●

● Jackson Falls

Old Trace ●

●Tobacco Farm/
Old Trace Drive

400 ● Sheboss Place

TENNESSEE

43

● Old Trace

Swan Valley ●
Overlook

● Fall Hollow
Waterfall

390

Meriwether
Lewis Site ●

20

Summertown ●

Hohenwald ●

······· Tour
▬▬▬ Natchez Trace Parkway

RATTLE AND SNAP PLANTATION

COLUMBIA TO MERIWETHER LEWIS SITE

Milepost Guide

TOTAL MILEAGE
Approximately 55 miles

TOUR ENDPOINTS
This tour begins in Columbia, Tennessee, and ends near Milepost 386 on the parkway.

407.9 **HIGHWAY INTERSECTION**
TN 50 crosses the parkway here, giving travelers access from Columbia, Tennessee. There are no gas stations on this portion of the parkway. If you need to fuel up, the town of Shady Grove, located on TN 50 approximately one mile west of the parkway, offers travel services.

407.7 **GORDON HOUSE AND FERRY SITE**
This site offers rest rooms, picnic tables, and a short hiking trail to the ferry site on the river.

405.1   BAKER BLUFF OVERLOOK

404.7   JACKSON FALLS
This attraction offers rest rooms, picnic tables, and a steep, nine-hundred-foot-long hiking trail.

404.1   DUCK RIVER OVERLOOK
This site offers a short hiking trail, rest rooms, picnic tables, a shelter, and a wildflower area.

403.7   OLD TRACE
A two-thousand-foot section of the original Natchez Trace is located here and can be hiked.

401.4   TOBACCO FARM/OLD TRACE DRIVE
A tobacco barn and farm are located at this site. A two-mile-long drive along the original Natchez Trace also begins here. This one-way dirt road, suitable for almost any type of vehicle, will deposit you back onto the parkway.

400.2   SHEBOSS PLACE
Picnic tables are available at this site.

397.3   OLD TRACE

392.5   SWAN VALLEY OVERLOOK

392.4   FALL HOLLOW WATERFALL

385.9   MERIWETHER LEWIS SITE
This well-developed site offers a ranger station, a campground, a picnic area, rest rooms, and historic monuments and sites. Grinder's Stand is located here. Hohenwald, Tennessee, is located approximately 6.5 miles west on TN 20.

The tour begins in the charming town of Columbia, Tennessee, located approximately fifteen miles east of the parkway via TN 50.

Visitors to Columbia's downtown square may find themselves taking a step back in time. Scenic, shady streets are lined by row after row of historic homes and buildings. While driving past them, you may see a young mother pushing her baby in an old-fashioned pram over uneven sidewalks. Or you may see a pair of shaggy dogs excitedly scampering across a green lawn, eager to spend a day tormenting the neighborhood cat. Or you may see thousands of mules filling the town.

Yup, mules. Columbia is well known for its antiques, historic buildings, and antebellum homes dating back to the early 1800s. In fact, it is considered the antebellum home capital of Tennessee. The town is also one of the stops on Tennessee's Antebellum Trail. But Columbia's most colorful claim to fame is its notoriety as the "Mule Capital of the World." Boy howdy, imagine that.

Back in the 1840s, Columbia became widely known for its street sales of mules. Traders came from all over the nation with their braying beasts in tow for Market Day, held the first Monday in April.

About one hundred years after Columbia made its reputation as a leading mule market, the event blossomed into a more festive affair. A parade and other activities followed the mule auction, and a tradition was born. Will Rogers was quoted as saying, "What the thoroughfare of Wall Street will do to you if you don't know a stock, Columbia will do to you if you don't know a mule."

Columbia's Mule Day celebration is usually held during the first week of April. It begins with the selling and trading of thousands of mules, much like the Market Days of the early nineteenth century. Over the next few days, the festivities continue with a parade, fiddling contests, barbecues, pancake breakfasts, and much more.

If you miss Mule Day, don't despair, for there are many more attractions in Columbia that are sure to pique your interest. Starting with Columbia's historic downtown square, you will be enveloped by vestiges of the past. This classic Southern public square is listed on the National Register of Historic Places. That comes as no surprise when you learn that the square encompasses nearly one hundred historic buildings, some dating back to the early 1800s. A walk down one of the streets will give you a hint of what the town was like hundreds of years ago. You almost expect to turn a corner to see the diaphanous figure of a Confederate soldier silently slipping past.

In addition to the historic churches, homes, and buildings, the downtown area is filled with restaurants and shops.

From Columbia's downtown square, turn onto West Seventh Street and drive 0.1 mile to reach the ancestral home of President James K. Polk. Located at 301 West Seventh, two blocks west of the Maury County Courthouse and across the street from the chamber of commerce, this historic home is open year-round.

A registered National Historic Landmark, it is the only surviving residence, other than the White House, once inhabited by the eleventh president of the United States. President Polk's father, Samuel, built this Federal-style home in 1816. James K. Polk began his political and legal career while residing under this roof with his parents.

While commander in chief, Polk was well respected for his many accomplishments. Though he was a little-known presidential candidate and campaigned to serve but one term, many scholars and historians consider James K. Polk one of America's greatest presidents. Perhaps his most notable achievement was the extension of the United States from the Atlantic to the Pacific, from sea to shining sea.

Visitors to the home can see a display of political artifacts, White House memorabilia, personal belongings, and furnishings used by the former president and his wife, Sarah. Sister's House Museum, adjacent to the house, features exhibits which trace Polk's career and life. The former president's inaugural Bible and Mrs. Polk's ball gown are also displayed in the museum.

The next stop in Columbia is the Athenaeum, located at 808 Athenaeum Drive. From the Polk home, drive west on West Seventh Street for two and a half blocks, then turn left onto Athenaeum Drive.

In a land of white-columned plantation homes and antebellum structures, the Athenaeum stands out like a sore thumb. This unusual structure was built in the Gothic Revival style, uncommon in the early-1800s South.

Listed on the National Register of Historic Places, the Athenaeum was built in 1835 as a residence for Samuel Polk Walker, nephew of future president James K. Polk. Completed in 1837, it later became the home of the Reverend Franklin G. Smith, who turned the Athenaeum into a school for girls in 1852. Widely acclaimed across the South, the school offered courses in science, chemistry, music, art, natural history, modern history, and ancient history. Sounds like an

THE ATHENAEUM

amazingly sophisticated curriculum for young women in the days before the feminist movement, doesn't it? However, the girls were also given instruction in tennis, croquet, and, of course, etiquette. After all, what good was knowledge of the fall of the Roman Empire if one didn't know where to place a soup spoon in a formal table setting? The school remained in operation for more than fifty years and finally closed around the turn of the century.

The Athenaeum has now been fully restored and is open to the public for tours. Maintained by the Association for the Preservation of Tennessee Antiquities, it serves as headquarters for the Majestic Middle Tennessee Fall Tour.

If you are interested in one more stop before turning onto the Natchez Trace Parkway, return to West Seventh Street and drive approximately 0.25 mile west to U.S. 43 South (Trotwood Avenue). Turn left and drive 7.2 miles south from downtown Columbia to Rattle and Snap Plantation.

Despite its undignified name, Rattle and Snap has the look of a quintessential antebellum home. It is the word *grand* brought to life. The mansion and landscaped grounds are vivid reminders of the days of opulence, when cotton was king in Tennessee. A National

Historic Landmark, Rattle and Snap is considered by some to be the finest restored plantation in the nation. With the exception of the marble mantels, which were imported from Italy, the entire house was built by American craftsmen. The lumber was hewn from local timber, the bricks were fired locally, and the massive columns were carved in other states and barged downriver to Nashville.

The governor of North Carolina acquired this land as part of a grant at the end of the American Revolution. Colonel William Polk's subsequent acquisition of the plantation was quite unconventional. It seems that Polk engaged the governor in a friendly game of chance called "Rattle-and-Snap," played with dried beans. The pot was hefty, with more than five thousand acres of prime land at stake. Colonel Polk won the game and gave a portion of his prize to his son, George, who later built the grand mansion. In memory of his father's streak of luck, George Polk named the plantation after the game of chance. With such high stakes, Colonel Polk must have risked losing something substantial if the governor had won the game that night. However, your guess is as good as anyone's, because history's lips are sealed.

Historical sketches tell us that General Don Carlos Buell ordered his Union forces to burn Rattle and Snap during the Civil War. The captain of the unit sent to torch the plantation went inside the home before his men set the place on fire. No one knows if the captain was drawn into the mansion to steal any remaining silver or other treasures or if it was simply fate that lured him in. But once inside, his eyes locked on a painting of George Polk and the Masonic ring on his finger.

Stalling the plan to burn the home, the captain reported his findings to his commander, who in turn reported them to General Buell. Almost immediately, Buell stayed his order to burn Rattle and Snap. It is speculated that Buell may have been a Mason himself and was acting on some link of brotherhood that transcended war. But whatever the reason behind Buell's decision, the plantation still stands today as a testament to the days of the Old South.

Considered one of the finest examples of Greek Revival architecture in the South, the manor house contains elaborate furnishings from the mid-nineteenthth century. The surrounding fifteen hundred acres of land include gardens, trails, and picnic areas available to visitors. And in true tourist fashion, a gift shop and a restaurant are located on the grounds.

Retrace your path on U.S. 43 toward Columbia and the intersection with TN 50. Turn west onto TN 50 to reach the Natchez Trace Parkway. Drive south on the parkway from Milepost 408.

Almost immediately, you will come to the Gordon House and Ferry Site. John Gordon, distinguished Indian fighter, defender of early Tennessee settlements, and good friend of Andrew Jackson, obtained over six hundred acres along the Duck River by land grant in the early 1800s. In 1803, he opened a ferry service at this spot on the river, an operation that continued successfully for nearly ninety years. Before that, travelers on the Natchez Trace could only cross the Duck during dry periods, when the river was low enough to be forded. With the arrival of the ferry, travel became much easier and much less dependent on season and weather.

Gordon and his wife eventually built a home, known simply as the Gordon House, near the ferry site. Constructed in 1817, it was one of the first brick homes in Middle Tennessee. Gordon died soon after the house was completed, but his wife stayed on until her death in 1859.

Today, the house is being restored by the National Park Service. This simple two-story structure facing the river is one of the few remaining buildings that were part of the original Natchez Trace. Current plans are to convert the vacant house into a National Park Service visitor center after the northern section of the parkway is completed.

Just south of the Gordon House, you will drive across the Duck River. Imagine trying to cross the river during the rainy season before the arrival of ferry operators like John Gordon. Those were tough, dangerous days.

After passing Milepost 405, you will arrive at Jackson Falls, located on the right. The falls were named in honor of Andrew Jackson, who frequently journeyed back and forth between his home in Nashville and the Louisiana territory.

One of Jackson's most memorable journeys was in 1791, when he had a song in his heart and a spring in his step. He had received word that a divorce had been granted to Rachel Donelson Robards, daughter of Nashville's cofounder, the late John Donelson.

Young, red-headed Andy had been sweet on Rachel for some time. He immediately sought out her mother to ask for Rachel's hand in marriage.

"Mr. Jackson," she said, "would you sacrifice your life to save my poor child's good name?"

"Ten thousand lives, madam, if I had them."

Jackson wasted no time in leaving Nashville and traveling southward on the Trace, bound for Natchez to take his future bride in his arms.

Later years saw Jackson traveling the Trace with less romantic intentions.

After providing the United States with the services of more than two thouand Tennessee soldiers during the War of 1812, Jackson got orders to disband his troops without financial reimbursement or much-needed medical assistance. Furious, he refused to disband or abandon his army until he saw his men safely back to their Tennessee homes. Funding the group's return trip with his own money, Jackson supervised the journey to Nashville along the 450-mile-long Natchez Trace.

Observing Jackson as he endured the hardships of travel and suffered lack of sleep to provide round-the-clock care for sick and dying men, his soldiers got a firsthand glimpse of their leader's set-jaw resolve and compassion. Impressed with his determination and fortitude, they described Jackson as being "tough as hickory." By the time he finally returned to Tennessee, Jackson had been dubbed with his famous nickname, "Old Hickory."

From the parking lot at Jackson Falls, you can hike down a steep, nine-hundred-foot-long trail that leads to the base of the falls. Cascading over glistening black rock into a clear pool, the falls are quite pretty. You may want to pack a picnic lunch to enjoy before hiking back up to the parking area. Or you may just want to lean against a tree, close your eyes, and relax where Andrew Jackson may have paused while traveling the Natchez Trace.

Duck River Overlook is located adjacent to Jackson Falls. Here, you can hike a gentle 0.25-mile trail that leads to an overlook above the Duck River. During spring and summer, the wildflower area located here is ablaze with colorful flowers.

Continue south on the parkway. A preserved section of the original Natchez Trace is located past Milepost 404. Following a ridge several hundred feet above the Duck River, this two-thousand-foot-long section of trail can be easily walked in ten to fifteen minutes, giving you a break from the drive. As you walk, imagine the weariness of early-nineteenth-century travelers who had to cover twenty-five or thirty miles of this path a day on foot or horseback. I shared this observation with my children, who were complaining about having to get out of the car and—heaven forbid!—actually walk a few steps on the trail, but they were unimpressed.

Two miles later, you will reach the Tobacco Farm and Old Trace Drive, on the left.

At the Tobacco Farm, the barn is representative of early-twentieth-century farms. Tobacco hangs to dry in season. Though the state of North Carolina normally pops to mind when tobacco is mentioned, Tennessee is actually the nation's third-largest producer of the crop. Most people think cotton is still king, but tobacco is Tennessee's largest cash crop.

The entrance to the two-mile-long Old Trace Drive is just past the tobacco barn. A lovely detour from the paved parkway, this pale pink road can be easily negotiated by two- or four-wheel-drive vehicles.

TOBACCO DRYING AT THE TOBACCO FARM

Dennis Coello

THE TOBACCO FARM

Winding through the forest under a canopy of deciduous trees, it leads traffic one-way through woods filled with bird song. Occasional pockets in the thick trees allow glimpses of rolling farmland and weathered clapboard farmhouses.

If you have a bicycle strapped to your car rack, you might consider pedaling this dirt road, especially on off-season weekdays, when traffic is light to nonexistent. Beginning from the Tobacco Farm parking lot, cycle down Old Trace Drive. At the end of the road, turn left onto the paved parkway and begin a gentle climb. After about 1.5 miles, turn left to return to the parking lot. The total loop distance is 3.2 miles—not exactly a training ride for would-be racers, but enough distance to get the kinks out of your automobile-cramped muscles.

Continue south on the parkway. A mile or so past the Tobacco Farm, you will pass the site of Sheboss Place. As the story goes, an inn, or "stand," located here once lodged Trace travelers who were in need of overnight accommodations. A woman by the name of Cranfield lived in the inn with her second husband, an Indian who spoke very little English. When guests stopped at the inn to inquire about overnight lodging, the husband would simply point to his wife and say, "She boss."

Stands sprang up along the Trace as the road became more heavily used. At the request of the United States government in the early 1800s, the Chickasaw tribe allowed the erection of stands on its land, with the provision that the proprietors must be Indians. Inns established at one-day intervals along the old frontier road offered weary travelers food, rest, and supplies.

At the beginning of the nineteenth century, the Chickasaws owned all the land in this portion of Tennessee. They ceded some land to the United States around 1805, then a larger tract in 1816. In 1837, the government finally forced them from the entire area to Indian territory in Oklahoma over the tragic Trail of Tears.

Continuing south, you will pass Swan Valley Overlook just past Milepost 393. You can see for miles over the treetops at this spot. During autumn, when leaf color is at its vibrant peak, the view is especially pretty.

The parking lot for Fall Hollow Waterfall is just beyond Swan Valley Overlook. A short paved trail leads to the waterfall. No excuses on this one. Granny can manage this easy path, even with her Sunday pumps still on. There is a wooden bench and overlook deck along the way for viewing the cascade above the waterfall. A steeper trail leads to the base of the waterfall.

Continue south from Fall Hollow Waterfall.

You will notice signs all along the parkway reminding you that this is also a bike route. In fact, it is an extremely popular paved route for cyclists, particularly during spring and autumn. I spoke to two gentlemen on bicycles who had stopped at the Meriwether Lewis Site for a break. They told me that they were pedaling from Natchez to Nashville on an annual fund-raising tour to benefit the Children's Home of DeSoto County, Mississippi. The younger of the two pointed to the other and proudly told me that his friend was seventy years old. Chuckling, he added, "I can't keep up with him. I guess I'm just not old enough yet." As you drive, please watch for two-wheel travelers and give them a wide berth when possible.

Near Milepost 385, you will pass the intersection with TN 20. The Meriwether Lewis Site is on the right at this intersection; turn right to drive to the ranger station for information.

Many famous men journeyed along the Natchez Trace during its peak period as a boatman's trail and its later days as a national road. One of the most famous travelers was Meriwether Lewis, of the famed Lewis and Clark expedition to the Pacific Ocean. After Lewis returned from his western explorations, he and William Clark were considered national heroes. As a reward, President Thomas Jefferson appointed Lewis governor of Louisiana, a land area reaching westward to the Rocky Mountains. His office was in St. Louis.

The explorer-turned-administrator soon met with problems. Some suggest that certain aspects of the governorship infuriated him. Finally, a refusal by the War Department to honor several of Lewis's bank drafts from his earlier expedition to the Pacific called him to action. Outraged, he notified the War Department clerk in Washington that he would soon be arriving to fight the refusal and defend his transactions.

THE MERIWETHER LEWIS SITE

TRAVELING THE NATCHEZ TRACE

Dennis Coello

FALL HOLLOW WATERFALL

In 1809, Lewis left St. Louis and traveled on the Mississippi River, bound for New Orleans with the disputed vouchers and documents from his expedition in hand. He reportedly planned to board a ship once he arrived in New Orleans and travel to Washington. Once there, he also hoped to have the accounts of the Lewis and Clark expedition edited and published.

Fearing the British who were reportedly near the mouth of the Mississippi River, Lewis traveled from the location of present-day Memphis overland to the Natchez Trace.

Though the overland route would take much less time, it would also make for an extremely arduous journey. So why did Lewis change his plans? He wrote in his travel journal that the heat troubled him and that he feared higher temperatures farther south. Some say he was anxious about rumors that England and the United States were on the brink of war. Reports of British warships off the Atlantic coast may have caused Lewis to worry about the safety of his papers. Though that decision may have saved his expedition notes, it cost Meriwether Lewis his life.

Lewis arrived alone late one afternoon at Grinder's Stand during a violent thunderstorm. Mrs. Grinder, wife of the owner, recounted that Lewis inquired about room and board for himself and the companions he was expecting later in the evening. Mrs. Grinder made the following observations of that stormy night: "He seemed distraught all evening, pacing back and forth, and muttering to himself. His behavior upset us so that my children and I stayed in the kitchen all night. Sometime after midnight I heard a pistol shot and then Governor Lewis screamed, 'Oh Lord.' And then there was another shot."

Lewis was found with gunshot wounds to the head and side. He died shortly afterward, his death being attributed to suicide. However, many involved in the investigation of his death found evidence of murder. Some historians have even alluded to a conspiracy among government agents in St. Louis, who may have been jealous of Lewis's friendship with the president and his other connections in Washington.

Alexander Wilson, close friend of Meriwether Lewis and noted ornithologist, traveled to the Natchez Trace several months after the tragic death. Wilson spent a good deal of time investigating the circumstances of Lewis's death and interviewing people, including Mr. and Mrs. Grinder. He finally left the area convinced that Meriwether Lewis had not committed suicide but instead had been murdered.

Mr. Grinder was later arrested and charged with the crime, but he was soon released due to lack of evidence. Though regarded as poor for many years prior to this incident, the Grinders soon moved away from the stand and purchased a large tract of land in western Tennessee, as well as a number of slaves.

Today, a monument marks the location where Meriwether Lewis died at the young age of thirty-five. A portion of the inscription reads, "Beneath this monument . . . reposes the dust of Meriwether Lewis, a captain in the United States Army, private secretary to President Jefferson, senior commander of the Lewis & Clark expedition, and governor of the territory of Louisiana. In the Grinder House, the ruins of which are still discernable 230 yards south of this spot, his life of romantic endeavor and lasting achievement came tragically and mysteriously to its close on the night of October 11, 1809."

If you wish to visit the town of Hohenwald, exit onto TN 20 after leaving the Meriwether Lewis Site and drive approximately 6.5 miles west. A description of Hohenwald's restaurants, accommodations, and attractions follows in the next chapter.

Campground

NATCHEZ TRACE PARKWAY

Meriwether Lewis Campground
Meriwether Lewis Subdistrict
Route 3, Box 368
Hohenwald, TN 38462
(615) 796-2675

Located at Milepost 385.9, this free campground has thirty-two sites and a centrally located water and comfort station.

Bed-and-Breakfast Inns

COLUMBIA

Oak Springs Inn
1512 Williamsport Pike
Columbia, TN 38401
(800) 377-2770 or (615) 285-2777

This log-cabin inn is located thirteen miles from Milepost 409, near Columbia. Built in the early 1800s, the inn has a kitchen, claw-foot bathtubs, fireplaces, and a balcony offering panoramic views of the rolling Tennessee hills. Pieces of the host's artwork decorate the walls. Rates include access to the grounds and the tennis court.

CULLEOKA

Sweetwater Inn
Campbell Station Road
Culleoka, TN 38451
(800) 377-2770 or (615) 285-2777

This farmhouse, built in 1901, is thirteen miles from Columbia, Tennessee, and five miles from Interstate 65. It has been newly restored to elegant perfection. A double wraparound porch provides views of the countryside. In the morning, guests pull up their chairs to a table set with crisp linens, fine china, and a gourmet breakfast.

Unique Dining

COLUMBIA

Marion's Restaurant
104 West Sixth Street
Columbia, TN 38402
(615) 388-6868

Located in downtown Columbia, this restaurant is housed in a restored home built in the mid-1800s. Guests can choose from Southern and French specialties. Marion's serves lunch, dinner, and Sunday brunch. If you can afford the calories, try a house favorite, the caramel chocolate pecan pie.

Bucky's Family Restaurant

   1102 Carmack Boulevard
   Columbia, TN 38402
   (615) 381-2834

Though not fancy, this is the place to go for down-home Southern cooking. If you are looking for a good breakfast spot, then look no farther. After devouring baking-powder biscuits dripping with spoonfuls of sweet blackberry jam, you will be fortified and ready to begin the day's tour.

Henri's on the Square

   34 Public Square
   Columbia, TN 38402
   (615) 388-3543

Popular in the South are restaurants that serve up plate lunches known as "meat-and-threes." Three vegetables, that is. The selections at Henri's vary daily but usually include fried chicken, meat loaf, roasted turkey, rice and gravy, macaroni and cheese, turnip greens, black-eyed peas, and butter beans. Lunches come with steaming squares of cornbread and icy glasses of sweet iced tea. Fresh fruit cobblers served warm top off the meal. I believe I have worked up an appetite just writing about Henri's!

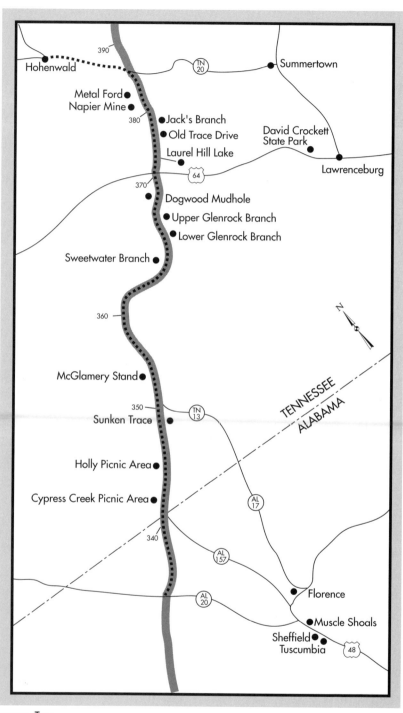

Tour

Natchez Trace Parkway

BRIDGE AT DAVID CROCKETT STATE PARK

HOHENWALD TO THE TENNESSEE/ ALABAMA STATE LINE

Milepost Guide

TOTAL MILEAGE
Approximately 102 miles

TOUR ENDPOINTS
This tour begins in Hohenwald, Tennessee, and ends at Milepost 337 on the parkway.

385.9   HIGHWAY INTERSECTION
TN 20 intersects the parkway at the Meriwether Lewis Site, giving travelers access from the town of Hohenwald. Begin driving south at this milepost.

382.8   METAL FORD
This site offers a picnic table and a short hiking trail that loops past an old millrace and an exhibit on the McLish Stand.

381.8   NAPIER MINE
Just a few feet from the parking lot at this site, visitors can view an open pit mine where iron ore was once extracted.

377.8 JACK'S BRANCH
This site offers picnic tables and rest rooms.

375.8 OLD TRACE DRIVE
Visitors can begin a 2.5-mile drive along a preserved section of the Old Trace at this milepost. *This section is not recommended for those with travel trailers and recreational vehicles.*

373.0 LAUREL HILL LAKE
This state wildlife management area, located 1.5 miles from the Trace, offers a campground, picnic facilities, and fishing opportunities. The campground is a little rough around the edges compared to Meriwether Lewis Campground and other parkway-managed campgrounds.

369.8 HIGHWAY INTERSECTION
U.S. 64 intersects the parkway here. Exit the parkway and drive approximately fourteen miles east to David Crockett State Park. The town of Lawrenceburg is one mile farther.

367.3 DOGWOOD MUDHOLE

364.1 UPPER GLENROCK BRANCH
This site offers picnic tables and rest rooms.

365.1 LOWER GLENROCK BRANCH
This site also offers picnic tables and rest rooms.

363.0 SWEETWATER BRANCH
This site offers a fifteen- to twenty-minute walk along a scenic nature trail.

352.9 MCGLAMERY STAND
A stand, or inn, was once situated on this historic site.

351.0 HIGHWAY INTERSECTION
TN 13 intersects the parkway here.

350.5   SUNKEN TRACE
       Three sections of the original Trace are located at this site.

346.2   HOLLY PICNIC AREA

343.5   CYPRESS CREEK PICNIC AREA

341.8   TENNESSEE-ALABAMA STATE LINE

337.0   HIGHWAY INTERSECTION
       AL 20 intersects the parkway here and leads east toward
       Florence and Sheffield. After approximately fourteen
       miles, it reaches the area known as "The Shoals."

The tour begins in Hohenwald, Tennessee, located approximately 6.5 miles west of the parkway via TN 20.

As you stroll the streets of Hohenwald, you may notice that the buildings and stores have a decidedly alpine look to them. This small town, whose name comes from the German word meaning "high forest," began as a German and Swiss settlement. Today, Hohenwald retains a certain Tyrolean charm. Even the local McDonald's has signs out front reading "Willkommen"—"Welcome." Local buildings are adorned with carefully painted window boxes that overflow with a riot of colorful annuals. Their ornate roof moldings and balconies call to mind Swiss ski villages blanketed with sparkling winter snow.

This quaint little town is a mecca for shoppers, especially bargain hunters. Secondhand clothing stores are in rich supply here. But if sifting through pile after pile of sweaters, trousers, and blouses sounds like punishment to you, then you may choose to skip the shopping spree in favor of browsing the Lewis County Museum, located at 108 East Main Street. From TN 20 West, turn right at the stoplight onto Main Street. The museum is on the right after approximately 0.2 mile.

Inside this natural-history museum, you will take a walk on the wild side, surrounded by trophies and full mounts of exotic animals from faraway lands. You will see African dik-dik, Marco Polo sheep, springbok, and gemsbok. After walking through a doorway flanked

HOHENWALD, TENNESSEE

by huge elephant tusks, you will see mounts of several Cape buffalo, considered the most dangerous game animal on earth. This ferocious beast would just as soon rip out a hunter's throat as look at him. You will also see wildebeest, hartebeest, deer, bongo, leopard, lion, and grizzly bear. So transporting are these exhibits that the distant beat of bongo drums and the steamy feel of Kenyan air blowing across your face would probably not surprise you at all.

Most of these exotic game animals were hunted by Nashville native Dan Maddox, an internationally acclaimed big-game hunter, and his wife. Maddox was also no stranger to the world of business. His successful professional reputation earned him a listing in *Who's Who in America* for ten consecutive years. However, Maddox never allowed the demanding cries of business to drown out the call of the wild.

The wildlife in the Lewis County Museum is said to comprise the fourth-largest collection of international specimens in the Western Hemisphere. Hailing from such distant lands as India, South America, Africa, Afghanistan, Mongolia, and Europe, each mount has a story of its own. Visitors not only learn about each animal and its habitat but also a little about the country where it was taken.

Next door to the Lewis County Museum is the historic Hohenwald

Train Depot. Listed on the National Register of Historic Places, it now houses the chamber of commerce. The depot offers displays on Hohenwald history, as well as tourist information.

But what if the weather is just too pretty to spend inside shops or museums? How do a few hours spent canoeing one of the last unspoiled rivers in the country grab you? If you are interested, then prepare yourself for a real treat, because Hohenwald is home to the Buffalo River, a paddler's paradise.

Picture yourself dipping a canoe paddle into tannin-stained water and pulling back against the river. Imagine your boat slicing across the still surface and creating a sound like silk being torn. Then, as you pause, all is quiet again. There is only the sound of river water dripping from the paddle resting across your knees. And maybe the soft murmur of conversation drifting from a companion's canoe gliding by.

Who doesn't love a flat-water canoe trip? Silently guiding a canoe down a still river may be one of the most sensual modes of travel there is.

The Buffalo River offers all of this and more. To gear up for a float trip down this beautiful waterway, contact Jim Hobbs through Buffalo River Canoeing. Jim has a fleet of about thirty aluminum canoes, along with paddles, life jackets, and just about anything else you might need for a day of canoeing. He believes that almost anyone of any age can negotiate a canoe on this slowly moving river. In fact, a group from South Carolina recently floated the river with Jim's help; one fellow in the group was eighty-nine years old!

However, if you are looking for the kind of crashing rapids and perilous runs portrayed in *Deliverance*, the spine-tingler that made the Chattooga River famous, you will have to look elsewhere. This is a float trip on *flat* water.

After drying off, it's on to the Natchez Trace Parkway. Return to TN 20 and drive east to the intersection with the parkway near Milepost 386. Turn right and proceed south on the Trace.

The next few miles of the Trace are beautifully rural. Cornfields and wheat fields decorate the parkway corridor. Wildflowers push up through green grass in a profusion of showy color. You will cross the tea-colored waters of the Buffalo River just before Milepost 383. As hard as it is to imagine, buffalo once roamed these lands and lapped this river water, hence the name.

Metal Ford is on the right after Milepost 383. The ford at this historic site was named for the rock on the bed of the Buffalo River.

There were no bridges during the early days of the Natchez Trace. Rivers and creeks had to be forded in shallow, narrow spots like this one. But during the rainy season, when rivers and streams swelled to flood stage, even the fords were dangerous or useless. As Alexander Wilson wrote in the early 1800s, "I was aroused from this melancholy reverie by the roaring of the Buffalo River which I forded with great difficulty."

In 1820, Steels Iron Works was located at Metal Ford. Pig iron was melted in a large charcoal-burning furnace whose machinery required river water for its operation. Though there is no remaining evidence of the furnace, visitors can still walk through the historic millrace that was used to bring water from the Buffalo River to the furnace.

The easy, five-minute loop at Metal Ford will also lead you to the McLish Stand exhibit. In the early 1800s, a mixed-blood Chickasaw Indian named John McLish operated a stand for travelers on the Natchez Trace. Though it is no longer in existence, the site where it stood is visible on the opposite side of the river.

The next stop on the parkway is Napier Mine, located just south of Milepost 382. Here, you can view a huge pit where nineteenth-century workers mined iron ore. Extremely rich in quality, the ore was comprised of a high percentage of iron. The mining process was crude. Workmen removed the ore from the dirt pit, and mule-drawn wagons dragged the huge chunks to a hammering area. There, men hammered the chunks into smaller sizes that would fit into the smelting pit of Napier Iron Works. Abundant resources and the demands of war kept the ironworks in operation for more than one hundred years. But hard economic times rang the death knell of the mine, which closed in 1923.

After leaving Napier Mine, you will pass Jack's Branch, on the left. This inviting picnic area offers a short trail leading down to a creek. Late-fall visits are especially beautiful here. Looking through the copper-colored forest, you will spot an occasional flash of silver as sunlight glances across the waters of Jack's Branch.

Old Trace Drive begins on the left near Milepost 376. This 2.5-mile road follows a section of the original Natchez Trace and

Dennis Coello

OLD TRACE DRIVE

offers a pleasant change from the paved parkway. Because of tight turns and a shallow stream crossing near the end, people with recreational vehicles and travel trailers are discouraged from driving this road. But those of you traveling in smaller vehicles are in for a real treat.

In autumn, when the surrounding forest is brightened with color, the drive is especially pretty. Springtime rides surround you with an explosion of delicate white dogwood blossoms, some close enough to touch, and the brilliant blooms of wild azaleas deep in the woods. There are several overlooks along the way that give a glimpse of the Tennessee countryside.

This lovely, narrow road is designed for one-way traffic only. Even without the posted speed limit of twenty miles per hour, you would probably want to drive slowly to savor the experience of traveling along this scenic stretch of the original Trace. A few pines and cedars dress up the winter woods with a splash of green, but most of the trees bordering the drive are deciduous. You will encounter a few rough spots in the road, but these are negotiated easily; a four-wheel-drive vehicle is not necessary.

If you care to do a little fishing, turn left off the parkway onto Brush Creek Road near Milepost 373. This road leads 1.5 miles to Laurel Hill Lake and the Laurel Hill Wildlife Management Area. As you drive in, you will notice a camping area on the left. Picnickers, campers, and fishermen are invited to use this 325-acre fishing facility, operated by the Tennessee Game and Fish Commission. A license and permit are required, however.

Back on the parkway, you will soon reach the U.S. 64 junction near Milepost 370. Turn left onto U.S. 64 East for a side trip to David Crockett State Park and the town of Lawrenceburg, the "Crossroads of Dixie."

It is 14.8 miles to the one-thousand-acre state park named in honor of famous Tennessee pioneer David Crockett. The park has more than one hundred campsites, each equipped with a picnic table and grill. There are also electrical and water hookups for those not interested in a primitive camping experience. The park offers bathhouses with hot showers, picnic facilities for day use, a paved bicycle trail, hiking trails, an Olympic-size swimming pool, and a restaurant on a hill overlooking the scenic, forty-acre Lindsey Lake. Live drama is occasionally performed in the restaurant by the Lawrenceburg Community Theater. Of course, the feature attraction in the park is the historic site of David Crockett's gristmill, distillery, and powder mill.

From the state park, continue east on U.S. 64 for approximately one mile to the town of Lawrenceburg, the county seat of Lawrence County. This town was named in honor of Captain James Lawrence, naval hero of the War of 1812, who immortalized the words, "Don't give up the ship!"

However, the man most closely associated with Lawrenceburg is Tennessee's favorite son, David Crockett. That's *David*, not *Davy*. When David Crockett is mentioned, it's hard not to picture Fess Parker and his famous coonskin cap. It's harder still to refrain from singing the lyrics to the Disney song from the 1950s, "Davy, Davy Crockett, king of the wild frontier." But nowhere in Lawrenceburg, or anywhere else, will you find this famous frontiersmen referred to as *Davy*.

Crockett was born in 1786, not "on a mountaintop in Tennessee," as the song suggests, but down in a river valley in East Tennessee, near where Limestone Creek empties into the Nolichucky River. We don't know if he actually "kilt him a b'ar when he was only three," but we do know he married Polly Finley in 1806. This lovely young woman soon gave birth to two sons. In 1812, she added a daughter to the growing brood. A proud papa, Crockett wrote, "I found that I was better at increasing my family than my fortune."

Shortly after her daughter's birth, Polly became sick and died, leaving her husband with three young children. Crockett later married a young widow named Elizabeth, who had two small children of her own.

Deciding that the country where they lived was riddled with illness and death, Crockett moved his family to present-day Lawrence County in 1816. The land where they settled had recently been ceded

DAVID CROCKETT MUSEUM

DAVID CROCKETT MUSEUM

to the United States by the Chickasaws. It was in this county that David Crockett began his political career as a justice of the peace. He went on to serve two terms in the Tennessee General Assembly and three terms in the United States Congress.

But David Crockett hit a political snag in 1835 that ultimately cost him his congressional seat. He voted against President Andrew Jackson's bill to remove the Indians from their land. This was a politically incorrect move at the time. Crockett reportedly told the voters of his district that same year that he was finished with politics for the time being, that they could all go to hell, and that he would go to Texas.

And to Texas Crockett went. And in Texas Crockett died.

We have all heard the story of the Alamo, but no one is certain just how David Crockett lost his life there. It is believed that Crockett didn't actually die in the attack on the Alamo on March 6, 1836, but was one of six Americans who survived. However, the six men were captured and taken to Mexican general Santa Anna, who immediately ordered their execution. When Crockett heard the order, he is said to have pounced on his enemies in a burst of fury, only to be attacked swiftly and killed with swords. His body was placed in the

TRAVELING THE NATCHEZ TRACE

center of the Alamo with the remains of those who lost their lives in battle and was burned.

You will find it difficult to wiggle in Lawrenceburg without brushing against some reminder of the legendary David Crockett. Even the town's movie theater is named after him. A life-size bronze statue on the public square depicts the famous Tennessee hero holding his hat and his trusty rifle, "Old Betsy." The statue was erected in 1922. To reach the public square from U.S. 64, turn right at the stoplight on Main Street. The square is only a block or two away.

There is also the David Crockett Cabin and Museum, which is a replica of the original office where Crockett lived and worked. The replica sits on the actual site of Crockett's home and houses books, pictures, and other memorabilia that belonged to him. This attraction is located one block south of the public square on South Military Drive, the road that the David Crockett statue faces.

Another museum in Lawrenceburg is the Old Jail Museum, located on the west side of the public square on Waterloo Street. This old, restored jailhouse displays items of local historic interest. Built before the turn of the century, it is listed on the National Register of Historic Places.

On the north side of the square, be sure to look for the Mexican Monument. When Tennessee was called upon for volunteer soldiers to help Texas in the Mexican War, Tennesseans responded in a staggering display of goodwill. Though only three thousand men were requested, more than thirty-thousand answered the call to arms. Ever since that time, Tennessee has been known as the Volunteer State. The Mexican Monument was dedicated to the memory of the volunteer soldiers who lost their lives in the Mexican War. It was erected in 1849, just a year after the bloody conflict.

The Mexican War wasn't the only conflict that saw a massive show of hands from Tennessee volunteers. The Civil War tested many Tennesseans who had mixed emotions about the war. That struggle of conscience is evidenced by the fact that Tennessee was the last state to join the Confederacy and secede from the Union. Nearly fifty thousand Tennessee volunteers joined the Federal troops. The majority sentiment stayed with the South, though, with some one hundred and thirty thousand volunteers joining the rebel forces, more than any other Confederate state. The clay soil of Tennessee saw some of the bloodiest action of the war—nearly five hundred skirmishes and battles. The only state to host more wartime engagements was Virginia.

Retrace your path on U.S. 64 from Lawrenceburg to the Natchez Trace Parkway. Head south on the parkway.

After all the talk of war and death, the parkway should be a pleasant change of pace. The setting is pastoral, with rolling green fields, hay neatly rolled into stacks, barbed-wire fences, and grazing cattle. There are now only a few more stops before the Alabama line.

Dogwood Mudhole is on the right after Milepost 368. About a mile south of this site, the early frontier path skirted a depression in the dogwood-covered flatland. During the rainy season, the area became a virtual mud bath, hence the name. Wagons could not get through, and travel on the Trace became extremely difficult.

Upper Glenrock Branch and Lower Glenrock Branch are located near Milepost 365. About a mile south of these picnic areas is Sweetwater Branch, named for the fresh, clean flavor of the creek's water. If you feel like getting a little exercise, you will be happy to know that a nature trail that can be hiked in ten to fifteen minutes is located here.

At Milepost 353 is the site of the former McGlamery Stand. This inn was established in 1849 by John McGlamery to provide overnight lodging and supplies to travelers on the Natchez Trace. It did not survive the Civil War.

Sunken Trace, an interesting section of the original trail, is located on the left near Milepost 350. Here, the constant pounding of early travelers' feet carved a deep, sunken path in the ground. The trail frequently filled with rainwater after heavy storms, which only furthered erosion. Huge mud holes would form, causing travelers to cut new paths through adjacent woods in an attempt to skirt them. As a result, a number of separate trails were formed in the area. At this site today, you can see three different cuts created by travelers attempting to avoid the mud.

Before reaching the Tennessee-Alabama line, you will pass two picnic areas. Holly Picnic Area is located a few tenths of a mile north of Milepost 346, and Cypress Creek Picnic Area is located just south of Milepost 344. Both sites offer picnic tables pleasantly situated beneath shade trees. The latter site is especially inviting, as the clear waters of Cypress Creek flow over a bed of crushed pink and tan rocks.

Milepost 342 marks the end of the Tennessee portion of the Natchez Trace Parkway. You will now swing through the northwest corner of Alabama as the Trace pushes ever deeper into the South.

If you wish to visit the area known as "The Shoals," exit onto AL 20 south of Milepost 337 and drive east. You will reach U.S. 48 in The Shoals after approximately fourteen miles. A description of the area's restaurants, accommodations, and attractions follows in the next chapter.

Bed-and-Breakfast Inns

HAMPSHIRE

Ridgetop Bed-and-Breakfast
P.O. Box 193
Hampshire, TN 38461
(800) 377-2770 or (615) 285-2777

This contemporary cedar home is located four miles east of the parkway near Milepost 392, very close to the Meriwether Lewis Site, Metal Ford, and Jackson Falls. The home is surrounded by 170 acres of wooded hillside dotted with sparkling streams, trails, and wildflowers. Large picture windows let you enjoy the scenery from the comfort of your room. You can sip your first cup of coffee of the day on the spacious deck while listening to morning bird song. If you have any questions about the local population of feathered warblers, ask your hosts; they are experts on area birds and wildflowers.

LAWRENCEBURG

Granville House Bed-and-Breakfast
229 Pulaski Street
Lawrenceburg, TN 38464
(615) 762-3129

More than one hundred years old, this inn is located near Lawrenceburg's public square. Five large rooms, all with private baths, are available. Some of the rooms have private balconies and some have fireplaces. Dinner is available at the Granville House by reservation only.

Unique Dining

LAWRENCEBURG

Bernie's Tea Room
212 Pulaski Street
Lawrenceburg, TN 38464
(615) 762-9229

Located in a restored home near the public square, Bernie's specializes in home-cooked foods. Each table is different, adding to the charm. This restaurant is very Southern in design, with honey-colored wooden floors and high ceilings creating a light, airy feel. Sun streams in through tall windows dressed in wide venetian blinds. The food selections are limited to daily specials, all very good. My daughter especially enjoyed the homemade lemon meringue pie.

Big John's Bar-B-Q
904 Military Avenue
Lawrenceburg, TN 38464
(615) 762-9596

This barbecue spot has been a Lawrenceburg favorite for more than twenty-five years. The menu offers barbecued chicken and ribs, vinegar-based coleslaw, and the like. Big John's makes its own barbecue sauce, bottled and sold in the restaurant.

Muscle Shoals

Florence

Sheffield

Tuscumbia

48

72

AL
17

AL
157

AL
20

Rock Spring Nature Trail

Lauderdale Picnic Area

AL
2

72

Tennessee River

340

TENNESSEE
ALABAMA

John Coffee
Memorial Bridge

330

Colbert Ferry

320

Tennessee River

Iuka

MS
25

72

Pickwick Lake

Pickwick Landing State Park

TN
57

Pickwick Landing Dam

Pickwick Dam

TN
128

TN
57

Savannah

TENNESSEE
MISSISSIPPI

N

······ Tour

Natchez Trace Parkway

INDIAN MOUND MUSEUM

THE SHOALS TO COLBERT FERRY

TOTAL MILEAGE
Approximately 50 miles

TOUR ENDPOINTS
This tour begins in the Quad Cities area of Alabama— Florence, Muscle Shoals, Sheffield, and Tuscumbia— also known as "The Shoals," and ends at Milepost 321 on the parkway.

Milepost Guide

337.0 **HIGHWAY INTERSECTION**
AL 20 intersects the parkway here, giving travelers access from The Shoals. Turn left onto the parkway and begin driving south toward Tupelo.

330.2 **ROCK SPRING NATURE TRAIL**
This short, easy trail leads hikers on a twenty-minute stroll along Colbert Creek.

328.7 **LAUDERDALE PICNIC AREA**
This site offers picnic tables, rest rooms, and a fishing spot.

328.6   JOHN COFFEE MEMORIAL BRIDGE
This one-mile bridge spans Pickwick Lake, part of the Tennessee River.

327.3   COLBERT FERRY AND STAND
This site offers a staffed ranger station, rest rooms, a picnic area, a swimming area, a fishing area, a boat launch, and telephones.

321.0   HIGHWAY INTERSECTION
U.S. 72 crosses the parkway here and leads 12.8 miles west to an intersection with MS 25 in Iuka. To reach the town of Pickwick Dam, Tennessee, turn onto MS 25 heading northwest. Take MS 25 into Iuka and drive 1.2 miles to a four-way stop. Continue straight on MS 25 for 18.8 miles; MS 25 becomes TN 57 at the Tennessee line.

The tour begins in Florence, Alabama, located approximately fourteen miles east of the parkway via AL 20.

Florence and the neighboring cities of Sheffield, Muscle Shoals, and Tuscumbia are known as "The Shoals." Straddling the beautiful Tennessee River, this cluster of cities is rich in recreation, history, and culture. There are a host of attractions, a handful of excellent restaurants, and several beautiful hotels and inns in the area.

With Florence only a hop and a skip from the Natchez Trace Parkway, it's no surprise that one of the town's main attractions portrays an aspect of Indian life. To reach the Indian Mound Museum, look for McFarland Park when you drive into the city. Exit AL 20 to the right past McFarland Park and drive under the U.S. 72 bridge. At the fork, bear left and follow the signs to the museum.

The Indian Mound Museum displays Indian artifacts and earthworks that date back some ten thousand years. This unique museum is filled with historical displays that are rated as some of the most outstanding in the South. The Indian mound located here is the star of the show, however. Forty-two feet high and 310 feet wide at its base, this domiciliary mound, called Wawmanona by the Indians, is the highest and largest in the Tennessee Valley.

POPE'S TAVERN

It is believed that Indians of the Mississippi culture built the mound sometime between 200 A.D. and 1500 A.D. Many such early Indian mounds served as ceremonial temples or homes to the great chiefs. This particular mound was surrounded originally by an earthen wall; villages and cultivated fields were nearby.

Many moons later, white men began to settle in this stretch of Alabama along the Tennessee River. Pope's Tavern, built in 1811, is the oldest structure in Florence. To reach this historic building from the Indian Mound Museum, drive north on Court Street to Hermitage Drive. Turn right onto Hermitage. Pope's Tavern is located at 203 Hermitage, one block from the intersection.

Built by slaves, this tavern was used as a stagecoach stop by early travelers and backwoodsmen. But during the Civil War, Pope's Tavern was no longer the place to stop for a pewter mug filled with cold ale. At separate times, it served as a hospital for Union and Confederate troops. It later became a private residence and remained so until 1965. Now, the city of Florence owns this old, black-shuttered tavern and has converted it into a museum. When you walk past the white columns on the porch and through the front door, you will find yourself surrounded by beautiful antiques.

The Shoals to Colbert Ferry

For one last stop in Florence, return to Court Street from Pope's Tavern. Drive south on Court to College Street. Turn right to see the W. C. Handy Home and Museum, located at 620 West College.

Back in 1873, this little corner of Alabama became the birthplace of a famous musician, W. C. Handy. As a boy, Handy would slip away from home and sneak down to the river to listen to the laborers sing. Their rhythmic spirituals mesmerized him. Their haunting songs, combined with the natural sounds of crickets, bullfrogs, and nocturnal birds, were a huge influence on the man who later became known as the "Father of the Blues."

Disappointing his father, who had hoped his son would follow in his footsteps as a minister, William Christopher Handy moved to Memphis when he was eighteen years old. During the difficult years that followed, he began composing the first of many blues classics. The famous "Memphis Blues" was born during this period. Later, Handy wrote "St. Louis Blues" and the immortal "Beale Street Blues." By combining his Southern black heritage with his early years of formal musical training, Handy eventually came to be regarded as a brilliant composer. His mournful, yet sometimes joyful, music strongly influenced another budding Southern talent: Elvis Presley.

W. C. Handy's boyhood home has been restored and is open to the public. The museum next door to the hand-hewn log cabin houses his original trumpet and piano, from which beautiful notes drifted so many years ago. A wealth of other memorabilia, including musical scores, is also found here.

Another famous person—Helen Keller—was also born in this neck of the woods. To reach Ivy Green, her childhood home, return to Court Street and turn right. Court Street soon intersects U.S. 72/AL 20. Follow U.S. 72/AL 20 eastward across the Tennessee River, heading toward the towns of Sheffield and Tuscumbia. After 1.2 miles, turn left to continue on U.S. 72 West. Drive an additional three miles, then turn right onto Tuscumbia-Decatur Road at the sign for Ivy Green. After 1.2 miles, bear left at the fork onto Sixth Street in Tuscumbia. Drive 0.7 mile, then turn right onto Dickson Street. After 0.4 mile, turn left at the stop sign onto East North Commons Street. Ivy Green is on the right after 0.25 mile.

If these directions sound complicated, don't despair; there are numerous signs pointing the way to Ivy Green.

IVY GREEN

Tuscumbia is a town of quiet streets and quaint white clapboard homes. Bright red geraniums add a spark of color to front porches lined with rocking chairs. Huge old magnolia trees preside over tidy green lawns. There are even white picket fences and creaking gates that beg for a touch of oil each time they are opened. Without a doubt, Tuscumbia is a quintessential small Southern town. What a shame it is to think that Helen Keller barely saw it.

Born a normal child in 1880, Helen became gravely ill with a high fever at the age of nineteen months. She nearly died. When the fever broke, her parents' joy over her recovery was soon bittersweet. They discovered that Helen was both deaf and blind.

Devastated, the family didn't know how to cope with her handicaps and ended up raising her like a wild animal for the next few years. Her mother would dress her in the morning, only to see Helen rip the buttons off her dresses and strip. She wouldn't allow anyone to comb her hair. Her table manners were atrocious. Refusing to sit down, Helen would wander around the dining room during meals. She had lost her senses of sight and hearing, but her sense of smell was keen. If she smelled something she liked—a link of sausage or a piece of fried chicken—she would lunge across the table and grab it from any plate she chose.

Her parents, Captain Arthur Keller and Kate Adams Keller, finally took her to Washington to see Dr. Alexander Graham Bell. He examined Helen and discovered that she was actually a brilliant child, just unruly. He encouraged her family to find a teacher for her. But who?

At the same time, a young woman named Anne Sullivan graduated from the Perkins Institute for the Blind in Boston. Anne had almost been blind herself but was able to retain her eyesight through a series of operations. At the age of twenty, she came to Ivy Green to take on the difficult task of being seven-year-old Helen's teacher and constant companion.

Anne Sullivan was not only kind and patient, but also quite ingenious. After seeing what a little hellion Helen was, she told Captain Keller that if she was going to teach the child, she would have to get her away from the family, who gave in to her every demand. However, Helen's father wouldn't agree to let Anne take her any farther than the little house adjacent to the main house. Anne was finally able to convince Captain Keller to allow her to trick Helen. Each morning, she would put her wild pupil in the buggy, and Helen's father would have them driven around and around the plantation grounds. Then the buggy would stop and Anne would walk Helen into the little house. For all Helen knew, she was miles away from home and her parents. Little did she know that she was in her own backyard.

Even after Anne managed to tame Helen a bit, there were still trying times. On one occasion, the mischievous Helen locked her teacher in the bedroom and hid the key. Captain Keller finally had to bring a ladder around to the side of the house and carry Anne down like a sack of potatoes.

A few years after Anne Sullivan's arrival in Alabama, she and Helen left for the Perkins Institute for the Blind. While attending school there, Helen also went to speech school. Anne was her constant companion through all those years and many more. Eventually, Helen was accepted to Radcliffe College, from which she received a degree at the age of twenty-four.

Those college years were trying times for both Helen and Anne.

Radcliffe, part of Harvard University, didn't really want Helen. It had no facilities for a handicapped person and no Braille textbooks. So Anne Sullivan had to stay with Helen around the clock. She went to class with her. She took all the notes. Then she had to teach it all to Helen. Without Braille textbooks, Anne had to instruct her in the manual alphabet. Anne's fingertips are said to have gotten so sore at night that she couldn't sleep. And what little sleep she got was often interrupted by Helen, who had no concept of time. She didn't know dark from daylight. And when Helen awakened, poor Anne had to get up as well.

After finishing college with honors, Helen traveled with Anne all over the world. During her adult years, Helen wrote fifteen books, which ultimately were translated into over fifty languages.

After forty-nine years of loyal service to Helen, Anne Sullivan died. Polly Thompson, Ivy Green's Scottish secretary, then took over as Helen's companion, remaining so until Helen's death at the age of eighty-eight. The three women are buried side by side in Washington Cathedral in the nation's capital.

When walking up to Ivy Green, be sure to notice the ivy winding up the huge magnolia tree out front; the tree has been there since 1820. Inside, you will walk across white-pine floors which are over 170 years old. The house is brimming with original furnishings and antiques that belonged to the Keller family. Some are quite interesting. In the hallway is a petticoat table. Back in the days of antebellum dresses, some of these tables had mirrors built into the bottom of them so that ladies could walk past and check to be sure their petticoats weren't showing. There is also a fainting chair, designed to catch swooning ladies. No, they weren't afflicted with a medical malady that made them lose consciousness. Their corsets were just laced so tightly that their circulation was compromised!

In the parlor, next to the fireplace, you will see a fire shield decorated with petit point needlework. In the days when the fireplace was the only source of heat in the house, the shield acted as a sort of thermostat. It was raised or lowered when the ladies' faces got too hot while sitting next to the fire or when the men's waxed mustaches started to melt.

Outside, you will see the famous hand pump where Helen learned to spell her first word: *water*. The small building that was used as a schoolhouse is also still standing. A brick walkway leads from the main house to the former kitchen, which, in accordance with the times, was housed in a separate building. Many such walkways connecting kitchen to house were called "whistle walks," and the Kellers' was no exception. To be certain the cook and servants didn't sample the food they carried from the kitchen to the dining room, plantation owners required them to whistle while they walked.

This property has been placed on the National Register of Historic Places. Built in 1820, Ivy Green was the second house erected in Tuscumbia. Sixty years later, Helen Adams Keller—America's "First Lady of Courage"—was born. This house and its adjacent structures memorialize the beautiful woman who inspired so many people around the world.

Ready to return to the Natchez Trace Parkway? If so, retrace your path back across the Tennessee River. Drive west on AL 20 for approximately fourteen miles to the parkway. Head south toward Tupelo.

This portion of the Trace is flanked by cotton fields. Late fall is harvest season, probably the best time to see the cotton in full bloom. From a distance, the fields don't look like cotton fields at all. Instead, they look like a light dusting of snow has fallen and sifted through the dull brown brush to rest on low branches. Of course, on closer inspection, that snow becomes loose balls of cotton still attached to their drying host plants.

The first stop on the Trace is Rock Spring Nature Trail, located between Milepost 331 and Milepost 330. This easy, relatively short trail with a crushed-stone surface takes about twenty minutes to hike. It threads through the woods and crosses Colbert Creek. As you gingerly step on the stones placed across the creek, look closely and you may see tiny fish darting about. The trail next snakes past Rock Spring, giving you a chance to explore a natural spring as it trickles up from the ground. The path then continues on a winding course through a heavily wooded hillside. During early summer, be sure to notice the wild strawberries intermingled with the undergrowth along the trail. Wildflower aficionados will enjoy identifying the many types of flowers growing in the forest.

Continue south on the parkway. When you reach Lauderdale Picnic Area, near Milepost 329, you will have a great view of the sparkling water of the southeast end of Pickwick Lake. This lake was

Rock Spring Nature Trail

formed by Pickwick Landing Dam, which spans the wide, majestic Tennessee River. The river begins in Knoxville, Tennessee, at the confluence of the French Broad and Holston rivers. More than 650 miles long, the Tennessee finally empties into the Ohio River near Paducah, Kentucky.

Though its calm waters don't indicate it, the river was extremely treacherous hundreds of years ago. Roaring, dangerous rapids were located all along its course, especially near The Shoals. But the Tennessee Valley Authority got busy in the early 1930s and built a series of dams and locks along the river. The result was a wide, placid stretch of waterway that bears little resemblance to the former whitewater river.

Lauderdale Picnic Area, with its expansive views of water, is a great spot to linger for lunch. Picnic tables and rest rooms are located here, as is a fishing area. This is also a good place to snap photographs of the mile-long John Coffee Memorial Bridge, which you will cross heading south on the parkway.

This impressive bridge spanning the Tennessee was named for one of Andrew Jackson's trusted assistants. John Coffee was a key player in the signing of the Treaty of Dancing Creek on September 27, 1830. With the execution of the treaty, the Choctaw Indians surrendered the remainder of their homeland to the United States. They were then forced to move west of the Mississippi River to the Indian territory in Oklahoma.

At the southern end of the John Coffee Memorial Bridge is Colbert Ferry, located north of Milepost 327. This busy site on the Tennessee has a ranger station, a picnic area, a swimming area, a fishing area, a boat launch, rest rooms, and telephones. A short trail leads visitors on a twenty-minute hike along a remnant of the Old Trace and down to the banks of Pickwick Lake. The trail also threads past the site of George Colbert's stand, which offered travelers a warm meal and shelter in the early 1800s.

Colbert was a mixed-blood Chickasaw who was once described by an itinerant preacher as "shrewd, talented, and wicked." He was an influential chief who negotiated with the United States for Chickasaw rights as the wave of white settlement advanced from the east. Thanks to Colbert's bargaining, Indians were given proprietary rights to all ferry operations on the Trace.

However, his negotiations were not entirely altruistic. Colbert had a keen financial interest in the ferry operations and quickly capitalized on the deal. Though his fellow tribesmen weren't aware of the identity of the donor, Colbert received a new boat for his ferry operation from the United States government. The government also gave Colbert and his brother, Levi, lump sums of money from time to time for their "help and support" with the Indians. It's likely that ol' George never would have reached the ripe old age of seventy-five had the Chickasaws known of the lucrative relationship he had with the big boys in Washington.

One of the most incredible stories about Colbert concerns an incident that took place in 1815. When Andrew Jackson and his army returned from the Battle of New Orleans and journeyed up the Trace, Colbert supposedly milked them for a whopping $75,000 to ferry troops across the river. Although this story has never been substantiated, with stunts like this reported about him, Colbert makes some of our more colorful congressmen look pretty dull by comparison.

Continue south on the parkway until you reach the intersection with U.S. 72 near Milepost 321. If you wish to visit the town of Pickwick Dam across the border in Tennessee, exit the Trace and drive west on U.S. 72. After about twelve miles, you will reach Iuka, Mississippi, a tiny murmur of a town named for a Chickasaw chief who made this site his permanent home. It is said that Chief Iuka was drawn to the mineral springs of the area, believing in their medicinal benefits. He stayed long after the faces around him grew pale. Never joining his fellow tribesmen in their westward move, Chief Iuka eventually died here.

Turn right off U.S. 72 onto MS 25 at Iuka and drive northwest; MS 25 becomes TN 57 at the state line. It is approximately twenty miles from U.S. 72 in Iuka to the town of Pickwick Dam.

Tennessee's Pickwick Landing State Park and Shiloh National Military Park and the town of Corinth, Mississippi, are covered in the next chapter.

Bed-and-Breakfast Inns

FLORENCE

River View Bed-and-Breakfast

Route 7, Box 1236
Florence, AL 35630
(800) 377-2770 or (615) 285-2777

This elegant contemporary home is located approximately nineteen miles from the Trace; exit at Milepost 337 or Milepost 321. Sitting on the Tennessee River, the inn offers breathtaking views of the river and Wilson and Wheeler dams. While breakfasting on the deck, you may spot sailboats, barges, and even beaver out on the river. Enjoy an afternoon nap in the hammock if you like. Some rooms have private baths and some have private entrances. Fresh flowers are a specialty here.

Wood Avenue Inn

658 North Wood Avenue
Florence, AL 35630
(800) 377-2770 or (615) 285-2777

Built in 1889, this magnificent Victorian mansion is located in the historic district of Florence just twelve miles from Milepost 332 on the parkway. Its wraparound porch, octagonal and square towers, ten fireplaces, fourteen-foot ceilings, and antique furnishings are sure to make your stay memorable. A full English breakfast is offered.

SHEFFIELD

Louisiana Kitchen

406 North Montgomery Avenue
Sheffield, AL 35660
(205) 386-0801

This New Orleans–style restaurant offers lucky diners excellent French Creole cuisine accented with a smattering of true Cajun touches. "This is *real* Cajun," says co-owner Buel Williams, "and not Madison Avenue Cajun." Matthew Wood is the Louisiana Kitchen's chef. He began his professional career in New Orleans at Antoine's and then moved to Restaurant Jonathan, where he presided for a number of years as chef of that premier restaurant.

After dining at the Louisiana Kitchen, you may find Scarlett O'Hara's famous words popping to mind: "As God is my witness, I'll never be hungry again!" The restaurant has been a Sheffield favorite for nearly thirty years. Twelve-foot ceilings, brick walls, and wooden floors enhance the charm of the building, built around 1883. Reservations are not required but are suggested.

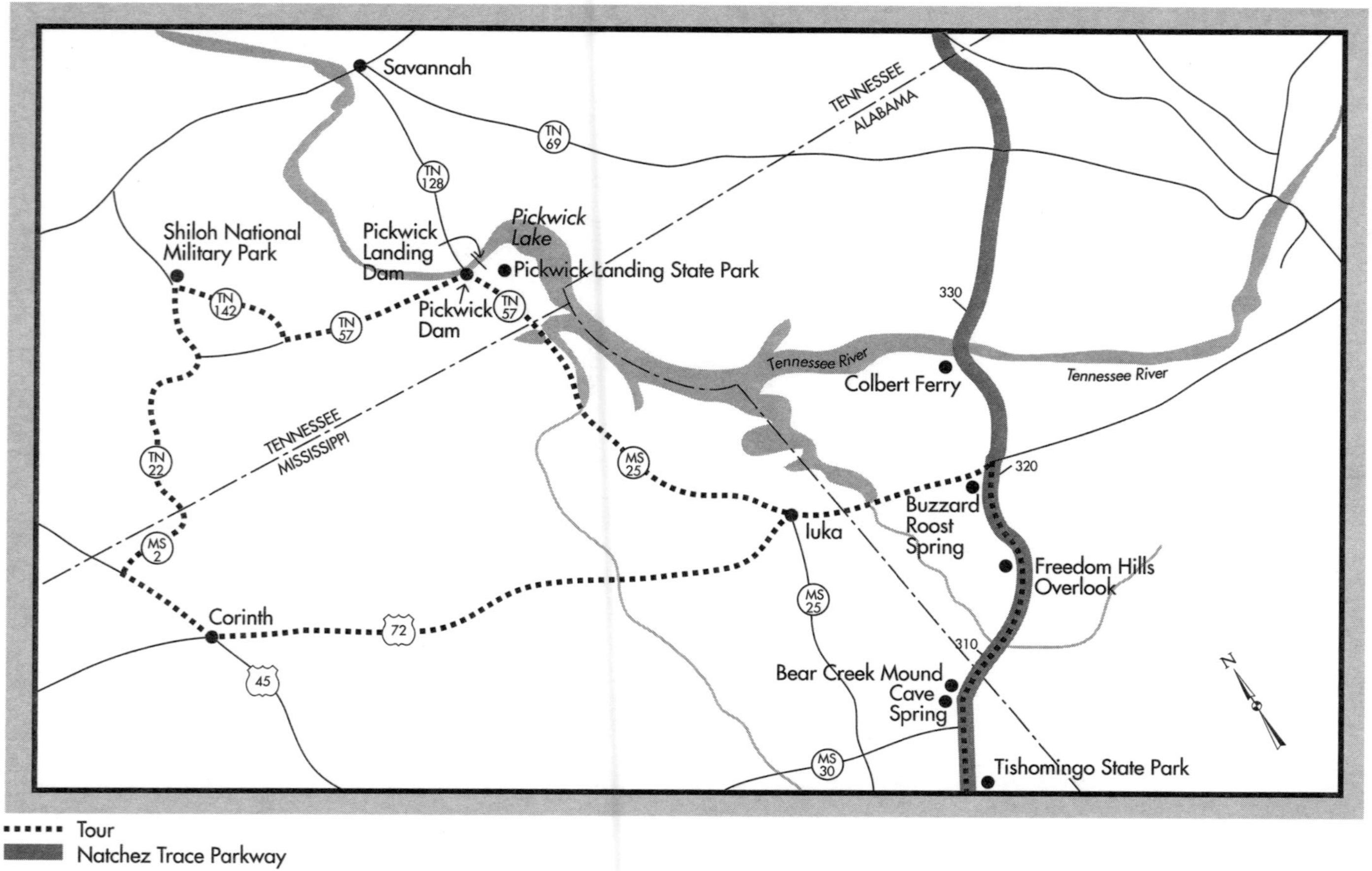

N

Tennessee River

Tishomingo State Park

Freedom Hills Overlook

320

330

Colbert Ferry

Buzzard Roost Spring

TENNESSEE
ALABAMA

Tennessee River

Iuka

Bear Creek Mound
Cave Spring

310

MS
25

MS
30

Pickwick Landing State Park

Pickwick Lake

MS
25

TN
69

Savannah

TN
128

Pickwick Landing Dam

Pickwick
Dam

TN
57

TN
57

72

TENNESSEE
MISSISSIPPI

Shiloh National
Military Park

TN
142

Corinth

45

TN
22

MS
2

.... Tour

▬▬▬ Natchez Trace Parkway

CAVE SPRING

PICKWICK DAM TO TISHOMINGO STATE PARK

TOTAL MILEAGE
Approximately 100 miles
TOUR ENDPOINTS
This tour visits three states, beginning at Tennessee's Pickwick Dam and Shiloh National Military Park, traveling to Corinth, Mississippi, and following sections of the Trace in both Alabama and Mississippi, where it ends near Milepost 303.

Milepost Guide

321.0 HIGHWAY INTERSECTION
U.S. 72 intersects the parkway here, giving travelers access from the town of Pickwick Dam and Shiloh National Military Park, both in Tennessee, and the town of Corinth, Mississippi. Turn south onto the parkway and drive toward Tupelo.

320.3 BUZZARD ROOST SPRING
This site offers exhibits which chronicle the tale of
Chickasaw Indian chief Levi Colbert, who owned a nearby
stand. A short trail leads to Buzzard Roost Spring.

317.0 FREEDOM HILLS OVERLOOK
This site offers a steep, 0.25-mile trail that ascends to an
elevation of eight hundred feet, the highest point on the
parkway in Alabama.

313.0 ALABAMA-MISSISSIPPI STATE LINE

308.8 BEAR CREEK MOUND
Here, visitors have the opportunity to see a ceremonial
Indian structure believed to have been built between
1200 A.D. and 1400 A.D.

308.4 CAVE SPRING
This natural spring is believed to have been used by
Indians as a source of water.

302.8 TISHOMINGO STATE PARK

The tour begins in the Tennessee town of Pickwick Dam, located
west of the parkway via a drive of approximately 31.8 miles. From
Milepost 321 on the parkway, head west for 12.8 miles on U.S. 72,
then turn north onto MS 25 at Iuka, Mississippi. MS 25 becomes
TN 57 at the Tennessee border; it is twenty miles from Iuka to Pickwick
Landing State Park, located at the intersection of TN 57 and TN 128.

Located on the shore of Pickwick Lake, Pickwick Landing State
Park offers excellent fishing opportunities. Visitors can also enjoy
swimming, boating, and water-skiing. Golfers can take advantage of
a popular eighteen-hole golf course. A full-service marina also is
located here.

From the intersection of TN 57 and TN 128, head north on
TN 128 a short distance to Pickwick Lock and the visitor center at
Pickwick Landing Dam; the dam is visible from the intersection.

Pickwick Landing Dam is an impressive structure built by the Tennessee Valley Authority. Completed in 1938, four years after construction started, the dam is more than one hundred feet high and more than seven thousand feet long. Once the dam was in place, Pickwick Lake began to fill with water, eventually reaching a length of about fifty miles. The dam thus created an important waterway for barges and towboats that would not have been able to negotiate the rapids of the Tennessee River. Today, visitors can watch boats pass through the dam's lock. They can also visit a museum featuring exhibits about the river.

From the dam, return to the intersection with TN 57 and turn right. It is 5.3 miles west on TN 57 to the junction with TN 142. Turn right and drive 5.4 miles on TN 142 to the intersection with TN 22. The entrance to Shiloh National Military Park is on the left just north of this intersection. Follow the signs to the visitor center.

Today, Shiloh is a quiet, peaceful place. The park is nestled in a pastoral corner of land that is old and gentle. It is laced with pretty roads that wind past tall, stately trees that seem to be guarding the park like dignified, grim-lipped sentinels. All around are markers and monuments that honor both Union and Confederate units. Row after row of gravestones pay homage to the many men who died in this important Civil War battle.

As you walk through Shiloh today, the only sounds you may hear are the whisper of wind tussling the high branches of trees or the low murmur of voices coming from park visitors crouched over tombstones. What you won't hear are the horrific sounds of battle that attacked the night air—the roaring boom of cannons, the staccato report of rifles, the cries of dying men clinging to their last moments of life. It is almost impossible to imagine those sounds in this pastoral place today.

This was one of the sites of the first major Civil War battles in the West. It was a brutal, bloody clash that gave both the Confederacy and the Union their first real taste of the horrors of war. It shocked the nation with the extent of the carnage.

In the days before the first shots of battle rang out, the Confederate troops of General Albert Sidney Johnston had fallen back to Corinth, Mississippi, under the assault of forces led by General Don Carlos Buell and General Ulysses S. Grant.

Pickwick Dam to Tishomingo State Park

As Johnston fell back to Pittsburg Landing on the Tennessee River, Grant followed him. While Johnston concentrated his forces in and about Corinth, Grant's forces moved down the Tennessee River and camped at Pittsburg Landing. Meanwhile, Buell was ordered to bring his thirty-five thousand men down from Nashville to reinforce Grant's fifty-eight thousand troops.

Johnston knew that he would have to move quickly to strike the Yankees at Pittsburg Landing before the two Union armies were able to converge and double their forces. A plan of attack was drawn by General P. G. T. Beauregard, who recently had been dispatched to the area to serve as second-in-command to Johnston. The plan was to move forty-three thousand troops to Pittsburg Landing from the fifty-five thousand Johnston had concentrated in Corinth. By April 5, 1862, the rebels were in position for the planned dawn attack the following day.

Beauregard expressed concern to Johnston that the commotion made by the troops as they moved into position may have alerted the Federals to their presence. His main concern was that once the Federals were alerted, they would be entrenched and prepared to meet a Confederate assault. Any attack made then would be suicidal. He was also concerned that too much time had elapsed, and that Buell and Grant may have converged already. But Johnston, excited and ready for the attack, stuck to the plan.

Beauregard's worries were for naught. Grant and Buell had not yet met. Additionally, Grant had no clue that the Confederates were anywhere nearby. In fact, he spent the night of April 5 at the Federal headquarters, housed upriver in Savannah, Tennessee, at the home of William Cherry. General William T. Sherman was on the ground, acting as senior brigadier commander while Grant was away. Three other divisions were also on the ground but Sherman led the forward division; to them went most of the security. Sherman did not expect action so soon from the Southerners and had not posted defensive lines around the troops' encampments. Little did he know that the rebels were less than two miles away.

Sherman, along with Ulysses S. Grant and the leaders of the other divisions, did not think defensive lines were needed. They obviously had some concerns of a Confederate approach because they doubled their picket lines. However, the Federals were not completely alarmed into a defensive posture. Though they were somewhat lax and a bit overconfident, the Federals were under strict orders not to prod the Confederates to fight. Henry Halleck of St. Louis had even admonished the Union troops to fall back if attacked, and not return fire until Buell arrived.

Before dawn, Union general Everett Peabody sent out a reconnaissance group to scout for Confederate movement. This act was a direct violation of Halleck's orders. However, Peabody was never disciplined for the action; he was killed in battle before 9:00 that morning.

Light action began early in the morning on April 6—around 5:30 A.M.—and continued for about two hours. Only occasional, sporadic shots were fired. So, when the Federal forces awoke, they began to prepare for a routine Sabbath. Shoes were shined to a spit polish and dress uniforms were pulled out for the Sunday procession. It was only as the Yankees were eating oatmeal and sipping weak coffee around 8:00 that full artillery began to roar. It wasn't long before reality began to sink in. The Confederates had launched their attack. General Sherman screamed, "My God, we are being attacked!" at the same moment a private at his side was dropped by a CSA bullet. Jumping for their weapons, the Union forces quickly formed defensive lines right through their camp.

Upriver, Grant had just roused from sleep when artillery fire ripped through the morning air. He asked that Buell's lead division move to the field to reinforce the Federal troops. (The remainder of Buell's men in Savannah were ferried upriver on steamboats later that afternoon and into the evening of April 6.) The troops under Sherman and Brigadier General Benjamin M. Prentiss were being pushed back from their positions, some of them even breaking from the line and fleeing from the Confederates. As Grant was riding along Corinth Road towards the hub of the action, his sword was hit with a piece of shrapnel just below his hip. Had it hit an inch higher, he would have been wounded seriously.

Fierce and concentrated, the center of the fighting was called the "Hornet's Nest." Even though a mass of Confederates under Johnston's direction swarmed around and attacked the Hornet's Nest at least a dozen times, the small defense of 6,200 Federals hung on.

Confederate attention was also focused on a growing number of

SHILOH MILITARY PARK

Yankees in a nearby peach orchard. Johnston led a heavy rebel attack against them, but the Confederate charge came at a high price. Johnston was hit by a Yankee bullet in the back of his knee, yet continued to lead his men in battle. Suddenly, he fell from his horse and died. The bullet had severed an artery, causing Johnston to bleed to death. Had he taken the time to apply a tourniquet, the bleeding probably could have been stopped.

Beauregard took over the command of the Confederate troops and blasted the Hornet's Nest. He put together over ten Confederate batteries (each consisting of four to six guns)—the largest concentration of artillery yet seen in battle in the Western hemisphere—and fired on Grant's men at close range. Union general W. H. L. Wallace, who was commanding troops on the right with reinforcements from Prentiss's flank, was shot in the head and presumed dead. However, he survived the injury initially and was taken to the home of William Cherry.

Ironically, Wallace's wife was traveling by steamboat to surprise her husband with a visit. She stayed at his side and nursed him, though he died four days later. Mrs. Wallace's father, two brothers, several brothers-in-law, and other distant relatives also served in the Civil War. Her husband was the only person in the family to die from injuries sustained in battle.

By late afternoon, Prentiss was prepared to surrender the combined troops of his men and Wallace's men (60 percent of the 2,200 troops were Wallace's) when the Union troops reorganized and formed a tough defensive line in the rear. The rebels, disorganized and weakened, were unable to launch an all-out final attack. Beauregard called off the offensive, certain that the next day would bring a rebel victory.

But when the first pink light of morning seeped onto the Tennessee horizon, the Federal forces were prepared to bring the Battle of Shiloh to a close. Buell and Grant had combined their troops, and two Union gunboats were lying ominously in wait. Simple numerical superiority on the second day of the battle gave them the edge over the Confederates. By early afternoon, Beauregard ordered his troops to pull back to Corinth, some twenty miles south of Shiloh.

When the bloody dust finally settled, the North claimed victory. But it was victory at a horrifying cost. More than one hundred thousand men saw the terror of battle firsthand, as their brothers and buddies and leaders dropped all around them. When the numbers were finally tallied, 13,047 Union soldiers and 10,699 Confederate soldiers were lost in battle. The loss of life at Shiloh was four times greater than the first battle at Bull Run.

After the battle, Union soldiers buried both the Union and Confederate dead close to where they fell. With the April heat bearing down on the bodies, this was the fastest way to bury such a great number of slain soldiers.

In 1866, the United States government established a cemetery at Shiloh for the permanent burial of Federal troops only. Their remains were uncovered from the battlefield and reinterred in the official cemetery, some grouped by regiment. Most of the buried soldiers are unknown. The simple tombstones bear either a number or the inscription "U.S. Soldier."

The Confederate dead were never exhumed and reinterred in the National Cemetery. However, after the park was established, five mass graves were located and marked with ceremonial rings of cannonballs and iron markers. In later years, the Daughters of the American Revolution erected other memorials.

The National Park Service has commemorated the battle with 150 monuments and nearly 500 historical markers. They serve to tell visitors why this area became such a bloody battlefield and to teach some of the history of the Civil War preceding this tragic clash.

Now, it's on to historic Corinth, Mississippi. From Shiloh, drive south on TN 22, which becomes MS 2 at the Mississippi border. It is approximately 40 miles from Shiloh to the junction with U.S. 45. Turn south on U.S. 45 and drive approximately 3.4 miles to U.S. 72. Turn east on U.S. 72. It is 1.8 miles to Cass Street. Turn left on Cass and drive 0.7 mile to the Corinth-Alcorn Chamber of Commerce. The chamber has mapped out an extremely interesting twenty-two-stop self-guided tour of Civil War sites. If you don't have time to see them all, you should at least try to stop by the major sites while you are in town.

Like a dramatic page torn from a Civil War history text, Corinth is a reminder of the war that pitted brother against brother and changed the face of the South forever. Though the major battle of this tristate corner of Mississippi, Alabama, and Tennessee was fought in Shiloh, Corinth played an important role.

Because it was at the junction of two major railroads—the Mobile and Ohio and the Memphis and Charleston—Corinth was the pot of gold aggressively sought by the Union and staunchly guarded by the Confederacy. Serving as Johnston's base for Confederate concentration, Corinth played an important role in the Battle of Shiloh. Its importance was immortalized by the words of Union general Henry W. Halleck, who told his commander, "Richmond and Corinth are now the great strategical points of war, and our success at these points should be insured at all hazards."

A month-long Federal campaign to seize Corinth began on April 29, 1862. Three armies advanced on Corinth in an effort to take the city under seige. After weeks of fighting, the Confederates finally evacuated Corinth on May 30. Federal forces moved in.

Beginning on October 3, 1862, the two-day Battle of Corinth saw fierce fighting on the town's streets, as Confederate forces attempted to drive out entrenched Union troops. Though many soldiers gave their lives in the valiant attempt to claim the town, their bloodshed was for naught. The Confederates were eventually forced to retreat again from Corinth.

A good place to start your tour of the kaleidoscope of attractions in Corinth is the Northeast Mississippi Museum, located on the corner of Fourth and Washington streets. From the chamber of commerce, turn left onto Tate Street. Drive 0.2 mile to a stoplight and turn right on Fillmore Street, then drive 0.5 mile to a stop sign and turn left on Main Street. After 0.1 mile, turn right on Polk Street. Drive 0.2 mile and turn left onto Fourth Street. The museum is on the left.

This railroad depot was built in 1919 to replace a depot that was heavily damaged during the Civil War. Tourist information, maps, Civil War artifacts, and exhibits on local history are offered here. The "Two Margarets"—Margaret Rogers, executive director of the museum, and Margaret Perkins, docent of the museum—are brimming with interesting tales of the past.

If you ask about the black mourning dress hanging in a side room of the museum, you will find out that it was worn by Sarah "Auntie" Carter, wife of Dr. A. W. Carter. The story goes that Mrs. Carter went to Battery Robinette the day after the fierce battle and, while there, recognized the face of a slain officer. It was Colonel William P. Rogers, the Confederate hero who led the third charge of the volunteers on Battery Robinette.

Mrs. Carter asked to remove his body from the battlefield so she could see that it received a proper burial, but her request was refused. The Federal commander had ordered Rogers's interment in the exact spot where he had fallen on the battlefield. This was a highly unusual order. Most enemy commanders order the dead to be buried in a mass grave, usually away from the battle site.

As Colonel Rogers's body was lowered, without a coffin, into the ground, Mrs. Carter placed her linen handkerchief over his face to protect it from the dirt tossed over him. It was the only bit of dignity she could provide as the body was laid to rest.

Depending on whom you ask or which history book you read, Rogers was felled by either one or twenty-two bullets. The Confederates claim that it took more than twenty bullets to stop this hero from Texas, while Union accounts claim that a single shot dropped the man. "Of course," drawled Margaret Rogers with a knowing smile, "we have to remember that the *victors* of the war wrote the history."

After you tour the museum, turn left onto Washington Street and drive south for four blocks to the stop sign at Linden Street. Turn right and drive 0.5 mile, over the railroad tracks and through a four-way stop to the crest of a hill. Battery Robinette, one of Corinth's most noteworthy historical attractions, is on the left.

Fierce combat occurred at Battery Robinette during the second day of the Battle of Corinth. The clash claimed the lives of 828 soldiers. The total number of men killed, wounded, or missing in action during the Battle of Corinth is 6,753. The Confederates suffered the most with more than 4,000 casualties. This battery was constructed by Union troops as part of an inner defense line only a few months after the Battle of Shiloh took place. It was reconstructed in 1976.

Another site you probably will not want to miss is Battery Williams. From Battery Robinette, drive east on Linden Street, returning to the four-way stop. Turn right. Just beyond the underpass, you will see Battery Williams up the hill on the right. A building now stands at the former site of Battery Williams.

Similar in size to Battery Robinette, this battery was armed with thirty-pounder parrot guns. Its cannon fired toward the railroad intersection that both sides fought so intently to control.

The next stop is Corinth National Cemetery, an impressive, yet chilling, sight. From Battery Williams, turn right and drive 0.3 mile to the blinking light at Tate Street. Turn left and drive to Fillmore Street. Turn right on Fillmore and drive to Cemetery Street. Turn right on Cemetery and drive to the stop sign, then turn left to reach the main entrance of the cemetery.

The final resting place of more than seven thousand men, this cemetery was established in 1866 by an act of Congress. Fallen

CURLEE HOUSE

heroes from the Battle of Corinth, as well as those from other battlefields in Mississippi and Tennessee, are buried here. Many of the grave sites are marked, but nearly four thousand remain unknown.

The last stop in Corinth is the Curlee House, an elegant antebellum home built in 1857. From the national cemetery, get back on Fillmore Street and drive to the intersection with Bunch Street. Turn left on Bunch and drive one block to Jackson Street. The Curlee House is on the right.

This home was originally called the Verandah House because of the porches that encircled it. The paint on this home had barely dried when the air around it filled with gun smoke and booming cannon fire. Though it was not destroyed during the Civil War, the Curlee House saw its share of activity. It was used by Confederate generals Earl Van Dorn and Braxton Bragg as their headquarters. It also served at a different time as the headquarters of Union general Henry W. Halleck. If only these walls could talk, what stories they could tell!

Today, the home is owned by the town of Corinth and serves as a museum. It is the only antebellum home in town open to the public

Pickwick Dam to Tishomingo State Park

on a regular basis. Inside, visitors can see the elaborate plasterwork, the original parquet floors, and the original gas fixtures. Beautiful antiques from the late 1800s decorate the interior.

To return to the Natchez Trace Parkway, turn east off Jackson Street onto Childs Street. Follow Childs to Cass Street and turn right. Cass will take you back to U.S. 72. Head east on U.S. 72. It is 31.5 miles to the parkway; you will reenter the state of Alabama en route. Head south on the parkway. You are near Milepost 321.

On late-fall drives, you may see dry leaves skittering across the road, the countryside a patchwork of brown-and-white fields of cotton cozying up to bright green fields of winter rye. The nearly leafless deciduous forests are accented occasionally by a clump of deep green belonging to a stand of evergreens.

After less than a mile, you will come to Buzzard Roost, the site of one of the most noted stands along the Trace. The inn that formerly stood here was owned by Levi Colbert, a mixed-blood Chickasaw and the brother of the infamous George Colbert. (For George Colbert's story, see "The Shoals to Colbert Ferry.")

Levi was a smart businessman who built his stand during a period when travel on the Trace was quite heavy. With the revenue from his inn, he was able to buy a good bit of land along the Trace, as well as mills and slaves.

In addition to being the site of Levi Colbert's long-gone stand, Buzzard Roost is also the home of a short hiking trail. This easy path leads to Buzzard Roost Spring, one of the many natural springs in this area.

Continue south on the parkway to Freedom Hills Overlook, a beautifully scenic site located at Milepost 317. Here, you can hike a 0.25-mile trail that leads to an elevation of eight-hundred feet, the highest point on the Alabama section of the Trace. The trail is fairly steep but certainly worth the effort.

As you continue the drive, you will see the rolling hills that stretch for miles in this northwest corner of Alabama. Late-afternoon drives are especially pretty, as blue shadows begin settling in the folds of these hills. Pine trees and rugged oaks dot these bumps in the landscape, which range in elevation from four hundred to nearly one thousand feet.

These are Alabama's Freedom Hills, the final remnants of the Appalachian Mountains, which stretch from the state of Maine down to northern Alabama before being swallowed up by flatland. No one is certain how these hills got their name. Some say the name is a credit to the free spirit of the people living here. Others suggest that it came from the freedom offered here to fugitives of the Confederacy during the Civil War.

Pushing deeper into the Old South, you will reenter the beautiful state of Mississippi—the Magnolia State—after passing Milepost 309. The road seems to flatten a bit more and the scenery begins to change, reflecting Mississippi's subtropical splendor, which has been sketched and photographed for centuries.

You will spot Bear Creek Mound soon after crossing the state line. This is thought to be one of the Natchez Trace's oldest Indian sites. It is believed that a village located here was occupied by roving hunters as early as 8000 B.C. The hunters were replaced by migratory Indians who settled here from time to time. They may have intermittently

COMMON FLORA ALONG THE PARKWAY

occupied this area for as many as one thousand years after the birth of Christ. Later, around 1200 A.D., agricultural-based Indians built Bear Creek Mound for use as a ceremonial temple for worship and for burial of their chiefs and religious leaders. They may have also used the mound to house their sacred objects and images.

Just south of Bear Creek Mound is the spooky Cave Spring site. Indians probably used the clean, clear underground water which formed this cave. It is believed that they probably used the cave for shelter, as well. As you approach the cave, you will be able to hear the faint trickle of water dripping from its roof. Green moss coats the ceiling of the cave, giving it a velvetlike appearance. Be sure to stay outside the mouth; signs warn visitors that the cave is unsafe to enter and the water unsafe to drink.

Continue south from Cave Spring to Tishomingo State Park, located near Milepost 303. A description of the park and the campground there is included in the following chapter.

Campground

PICKWICK DAM

Pickwick Landing State Park
TN 57
Pickwick Dam, TN 38365
(901) 689-3135

This park offers campsites, cabins, and picnic areas. An inn and a restaurant are also located on the property.

Bed-and-Breakfast Inns

CHEROKEE

Easterwood House
200 Easterwood Street
Cherokee, AL 35616
(800) 377-2770 or (615) 285-2777

This dignified old home is located just three miles east of Milepost 320 on the Trace. Burned down during the Civil War and rebuilt at the turn of the century, this charming home is nestled among twelve acres of giant old cedar trees. It was recently redecorated and is furnished with beautiful antiques. You may want to enjoy a glass of wine before dinner on the relaxing porch. Watersports enthusiasts will be interested to learn that this house is only four miles from Pickwick Lake on the Tennessee River.

CORINTH

The General's Quarters
924 Filmore Street
Corinth, MS 38834
(800) 377-2770 or (615) 285-2777

This inn, built in the 1870s, is located right in the heart of the old Civil War town of Corinth, close to Battery Robinette and the site of Fort Williams. Shiloh National Military Park is not far away. Four rooms with private baths are available. You also can enjoy a full Southern breakfast before you begin your day of touring.

Robbin's Nest
1523 Shiloh Road
Corinth, MS 38834
(800) 377-2770 or (615) 285-2777

This Southern Colonial home was built around 1870. It is nestled among two acres of dogwood trees, boxwoods, and azaleas in historic Corinth. Guests can relax on the back porch in antique wicker furniture. Ceiling fans on the veranda make warm evenings pleasant. Afternoon tea is served compliments of the house, and refreshments are offered upon arrival.

Unique Lodging

PICKWICK DAM

Pickwick Landing State Park Inn
TN 57
Pickwick Dam, TN 38365
(901) 689-3135

This modern hotel offers amenities such as a swimming pool, a playground, a gift shop, a tennis court, and a restaurant. A beautiful view of Pickwick Lake makes the inn especially appealing.

Unique Dining

PICKWICK DAM

Broken Spoke Restaurant
TN 57
Pickwick Dam, TN 38365
(901) 689-3487

This restaurant has been serving up plates of fried catfish and grilled steaks for almost fifty years. The decor is charming. Antiques surround diners, and candles are lit in the evening. You will find it difficult to resist ending your meal with one of the desserts; they are all homemade.

CORINTH

White Trolley Cafe

U.S. 72 East
Corinth, MS 38834
(601) 287-4593

This Corinth favorite is famous for its Slugburgers, a creation born during the Great Depression. No, they are not named for that slimy garden nuisance whose existence you curse every summer. Instead, their name calls to mind the slang term for a counterfeit coin. As you might expect, these sandwiches are not genuine burgers. Ground beef is combined with breading, and the patties are then deep-fried. Folks love them.

The day I visited the White Trolley Cafe, my daughter and I slid onto green vinyl barstools at the far end of the restaurant. Scanning the overhead menu, I asked the waitress about their Slugburgers. An incredulous young man seated next to me asked, "You've never had Slugburgers before?" When I shook my head, he recoiled and with slightly disdainful eyes asked, "Where you from?" Obviously, anyone who had never eaten a Slugburger was not from this fellow's neck of Mississippi woods.

We chatted until my Slugburger arrived, with pickles and onion, served on a sheet of wax paper. After sliding it toward me, the waitress stepped back to wait for my reaction. Another waitress joined her, and the two watched expectantly as I took a bite of the sandwich. "Delicious!" I pronounced. With pleased hints of smiles giving away their delight, they turned to check on their other customers. The young man seated next to me said, "Good, huh? Well, I guess they won't kill you. I've been eatin' Slugburgers since I was a little boy."

Country Kitchen No. 2

516 Fillmore Street
Corinth, MS 38834
(601) 287-8108

This is the local spot for breakfast. Country Kitchen No. 2 also serves up "meat-and-threes" for lunch on weekdays.

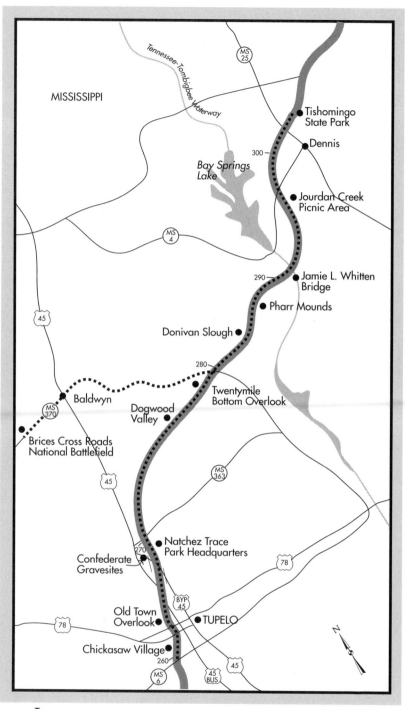

MISSISSIPPI

Tennessee-Tombigbee Waterway

Bay Springs Lake

MS 25

Tishomingo State Park

Dennis

300

Jourdan Creek Picnic Area

MS 4

290

Jamie L. Whitten Bridge

Pharr Mounds

Donivan Slough

MS 45

280

Baldwyn

MS 370

Twentymile Bottom Overlook

Dogwood Valley

Brices Cross Roads National Battlefield

45

MS 363

Natchez Trace Park Headquarters

Confederate Gravesites

270

78

Old Town Overlook

BYP 45

TUPELO

Chickasaw Village

78

260

MS 6

45 BUS

45

N

•••••• Tour
Natchez Trace Parkway

GRAVES OF THIRTEEN UNKNOWN CONFEDERATE SOLDIERS

TISHOMINGO STATE PARK TO CHICKASAW VILLAGE

Milepost Guide

TOTAL MILEAGE
Approximately 75 miles

TOUR ENDPOINTS
This tour begins at Mississippi's Tishomingo State Park and ends near Milepost 260.

302.8   TISHOMINGO STATE PARK
Named for a famous Chickasaw chief, this park offers camping, picnicking, swimming, canoeing, and fishing.

296.0   JOURDAN CREEK PICNIC AREA

293.4   BAY SPRINGS LAKE
An access to the lake and dam is located at this site.

293.2   TENNESSEE-TOMBIGBEE WATERWAY AND JAMIE L. WHITTEN BRIDGE

Picnic tables and a short walking path that leads to the waterway are located at this site.

286.7   PHARR MOUNDS
Rest rooms are available here.

283.3   DONIVAN SLOUGH
This site offers a twenty-minute hiking trail.

280.0   BRICES CROSS ROADS NATIONAL BATTLEFIELD SITE
Exit the parkway onto MS 370 to reach the battlefield. Precise directions follow in the text.

278.4   TWENTYMILE BOTTOM OVERLOOK
There is no circular drive here, so you may wish to forgo this overlook if you have a recreational vehicle.

275.2   DOGWOOD VALLEY
This site offers a fifteen-minute hiking trail through a stand of unusually large dogwood trees.

269.4   CONFEDERATE GRAVE SITES
A five-minute trail leads to the graves of thirteen unknown soldiers.

266.0   NATCHEZ TRACE PARKWAY HEADQUARTERS AND VISITOR CENTER
This site offers exhibits, information, books, a short interpretational film, and rest rooms. There is also a twenty-minute hiking trail that leads visitors through an area of forest regrowth.

263.9   OLD TOWN OVERLOOK

261.8   CHICKASAW VILLAGE
A fifteen-minute nature trail is offered at this site.

259.7   HIGHWAY INTERSECTION
MS 6 intersects the parkway here, giving easy access to
Tupelo.

The tour begins at Tishomingo State Park, located at Milepost
302.8 on the Natchez Trace Parkway.

Named for a great Chickasaw Indian chief, this park is considered
the most beautiful in Mississippi. The terrain is slightly hilly, and the
woods and meadows are thick with wildflowers and lush ferns. There
are stunning rock outcroppings and streams and creeks that thread
the hills like silver strings of mercury. Built in the late 1930s,
Tishomingo is one of Mississippi's first and finest parks. It offers
camping sites and rental cabins, as well as canoe rental for floating
Bear Creek. Though the park was heavily damaged by ice in the
spring of 1994, time is gradually healing the landscape.

Drive south on the parkway. The first site you will reach is Jourdan
Creek Picnic Area, located at Milepost 296. A number of picnic tables
are located on the banks of scenic, slowly moving Jourdan Creek.

Located a few miles south of Jourdan Creek is another body of
water. However, this one—Bay Springs Lake—is far more impressive. The access to this popular recreational site is located between
Mileposts 294 and 293. Boating, fishing, swimming, and camping
are all available here. There is also a visitor center, one mile west of
the parkway, that can provide you with more information.

Next, you will cross the Tennessee-Tombigbee Waterway, known
to locals as the "Tenn-Tom." Built by the United States Army Corps
of Engineers in the 1970s, this man-made canal links the Tennessee
River with the Tombigbee River. Its construction eliminated hundreds of miles of travel by providing a more direct route to the Gulf
of Mexico. A remarkable engineering feat, the waterway is more than
two hundred miles long, three hundred feet wide, and nine feet deep.

Off to the right, you will see the Bay Springs combination lock
and dam. With a drop of nearly ninety feet, this is the highest lock
on the Tenn-Tom. All told, there are ten combination locks and
dams used to control water flow and traffic along the canal. To get a
closer look at this lock in action, take the Bay Springs Lake access off

the parkway, located approximately 0.5 mile north of the Tenn-Tom Waterway.

Continuing south on the parkway, you will now find yourself driving across the Tenn-Tom on the Jamie L. Whitten Bridge, named in honor of a United States congressman from Mississippi. Whitten has been given credit for convincing Congress to appropriate funds for the completion of the Natchez Trace Parkway and the construction of the Tenn-Tom Waterway.

From the bridge, you will be able to see the structure housing the Corps of Engineers.

South of Milepost 287 is one of the most important archaeological sites in northern Mississippi, Pharr Mounds. And with eight dome-shaped mounds encompassing ninety acres—an area the size of one hundred football fields—it is also the largest archaeological site.

These mounds, which originated about 100 B.C., were built by Indians during the Woodland Period, which spanned the years from 500 B.C. to 1000 A.D. Once mostly nomadic, Indians began to settle in permanent villages during the early years of the Woodland Period. They continued to hunt and gather the abundant nuts and fruits found nearby, though their spears were eventually replaced by bows and arrows. Agriculture began to play a much more important role than it had in the past.

But the Woodland Indians' primary claim to fame is their mounds. In fact, they are known as the "Mound Builders." The odd structures you will see at Pharr Mounds are evidence of their keen interest in burial rituals. Archaeologists believe that the mounds were built by villagers who doggedly hauled load after load of soil and piled it up until a proper height was reached. Important tribe members such as chiefs and great warriors were buried in the mounds during this process. These age-old earthworks still have a fascinating appeal.

After cresting the hill below Pharr Mounds, you will drop into an area of bottom land known as Browns Bottom; there is a parking area on the east side of the parkway. During the early days of the Trace, when bridges were still unheard of in this undeveloped wilderness, this area was frequently wet and difficult to travel.

Below Milepost 284, you will pass Donivan Slough, located on the west side of the Trace. Here, a fifteen- to twenty-minute nature trail winds through a moist lowland area, or slough. The rich soil

DONIVAN SLOUGH

Tishomingo State Park to Chickasaw Village

and abundant water of this area provide ideal growing conditions for water oak, tulip poplar, and sycamore trees. A swampy channel cuts a winding path through this bottom land and supports the reigning patriarch of the slough: the bald cypress.

If you care to take a side trip to Brices Cross Roads National Battlefield Site, exit the parkway onto MS 370 near Milepost 280 and drive 8.6 miles toward Baldwyn. Turn left to stay on MS 370, then drive an additional 2.3 miles to a stop sign. Turn left; it is about forty yards to a stoplight. Turn right. It is 5.4 miles to the battlefield site, located on the right.

The Battle of Brices Cross Roads, which took place in this area on June 10, 1864, gave evidence of the brilliant tactical abilities of General Nathan Bedford Forrest. Overcoming humble beginnings, this illiterate farm boy became a wealthy man while he was still in his thirties. Forrest enlisted in the Confederate army as a private one month before his fortieth birthday. By the middle of the following year, he was a brigadier general.

BRICES CROSS ROADS NATIONAL BATTLEFIELD SITE

Though he lacked formal military training, he was considered a gifted officer because of his abilities to fight hard and move quickly. His basic objective during the war was to be the first to arrive at a battle position and to have the most men. Though these objectives were not always met, his daring decisions, strong leadership, and enterprising personality often gave him the upper hand. In fact, Union generals and officers were known to refer to him as "that devil Forrest!"

During the spring of 1864, General William T. Sherman was making his way through Georgia with plans to occupy and destroy Atlanta. From there, he would move on to Savannah and Charleston. The Confederate high command was well aware of Sherman's dependence on the railroad from Nashville to Chattanooga, his main source of supplies. With that in mind, General Forrest was ordered to destroy the supply line to thwart Sherman's Atlanta campaign.

When Sherman learned of this plan, he ordered General Samuel D. Sturgis to northern Mississippi to find and stop Forrest before he reached the railroad. Scouts informed Forrest on the evening of June 9 that Sturgis was concentrating his eight thousand men about ten miles from Brices Cross Roads. Though Forrest was outnumbered by some forty-five hundred men, he decided to move quickly and attack Sturgis's army.

Both men began moving their troops at dawn on June 10. However, the Union men reached and passed Brices before the Confederates arrived. Traveling along Baldwyn Road, Forrest ran into Federal patrols about a mile from the crossroads. His soldiers stopped the Union advance.

By midday, after reinforcements arrived, they were attacking Sturgis's troops with a vengeance. Forrest and his men were unrelenting. By early afternoon, they had pushed the Union troops back to Brices Cross Roads. Finally withdrawing, Sturgis and his men met with a stroke of bad luck when a supply wagon overturned at the Tishomingo Creek Bridge, blocking their only escape route. With the rebel boys nipping at their heels, the Union soldiers began to panic, trying to run and swim away. In the chaos that ensued, the scene turned into a bloody beating. More than fifteen hundred Union soldiers were taken prisoner, and seven hundred men were killed or wounded. General Samuel D. Sturgis and his men were soundly defeated.

After your visit to Brices Cross Roads National Battlefield Site, retrace your path on MS 370 to the Natchez Trace Parkway. The backroads scenery offered by this Mississippi highway is highly enjoyable. You will pass fields of fluffy sheep and even fields of fluffy cotton. On one of my trips down this country road, I found myself following a rickety old truck whose specks of green paint hinted at its former color, obliterated years ago by rust. The bed of the truck was fitted with a wire crib brimming with harvested cotton bolls. Wisps of cotton caught in the wind sailed through the air toward my windshield. The airborne cotton looked much like snow flurries, an odd sight on a balmy autumn afternoon.

Continue south on the Natchez Trace Parkway from Milepost 280. The next site of interest is Twentymile Bottom Overlook, near Milepost 278. The low-lying land of Twentymile Creek is visible from the overlook. This area is typical of much of the bottom land that the Trace passed through years ago.

Near this area stood an inn called Old Factor's Stand. The Reverend John Johnson stayed overnight at this stand in 1812 and wrote the following account, which testifies to the difficulty of travel on the Trace in those days: "I have this day swam my horse five times, bridged one creek, forded several others, beside the swamp we had to wade through. At night we had a shower of rain, took up my usual lodging on the ground in the company of several Indians."

The next stop is Dogwood Valley, located near Milepost 275. If you want to get out of your car and stretch your legs, a trail located here will lead you on a fifteen-minute walk along a sunken portion of the Old Trace and through a wooded area called Dogwood Valley. As the name suggests, this area has a dense stand of unusually large dogwood trees. You will especially enjoy this site if you are traveling in early spring, when the trees are in full bloom with a mosaic of beautiful white flowers. Dogwoods—the crown jewel of Southern trees—are almost always in bloom by Easter. In fact, they are as much a part of the Easter season as little girls in bonnets, colored eggs, and chocolate rabbits.

Thirteen Confederate soldiers are buried near the Old Trace between Mileposts 270 and 269. A five-minute trail leads to the markers, erected by the National Park Service. Each is inscribed with the simple words "Unknown Confederate Soldier." These plain grave-

GRAVE OF UNKNOWN CONFEDERATE SOLDIER

stones face backwards toward the Trace, where, more than one hundred years ago, these men probably left hobnail tracks in the soft dirt.

Who were these soldiers? Some say they fought at the Battle of Shiloh. Others say they helped General Nathan Bedford Forrest turn back the Federal troops. Still others say they were killed while defending the Tupelo headquarters of J. B. Hood's Army of Tennessee during the waning days of the Civil War. Chances are we will never know.

The Natchez Trace Parkway Headquarters and Visitor Center is located at Milepost 266 on the east side of the parkway. Here, you will find friendly, knowledgeable park rangers and personnel able to answer almost any questions you have related to the Trace. In the course of writing several guidebooks, I have had the opportunity to visit quite a few ranger stations, visitor centers, and park offices. I honestly can say that I have never found any of them to be staffed with so many kind and helpful men and women as the Natchez Trace Parkway Headquarters.

An excellent bookstore is housed in the visitor center. This is the place to pick up literature, tapes, postcards, and other items pertaining to the Natchez Trace, the Civil War, and regional history. A twelve-minute slide presentation on the Trace is played on request. Indian artifacts recovered from the Trace and equipment used by the Kaintucks are on display here. There is even a model of the kind of flatboat used to float goods down the Mississippi River to Natchez. Sorghum, soybeans, and cotton grow in a garden out front.

A paved loop trail, Beech Spring Trail, is located at the visitor center. It is an easy path that takes only about fifteen to twenty minutes to walk.

The trailhead for a hiking trail leading to Old Town Overlook—the next stop on the parkway—is also located here. This trail eventually ends at Chickasaw Village, several miles south of here.

Rest rooms and other service facilities are also found at the parkway headquarters.

As you head south from the Natchez Trace Parkway Headquarters and Visitor Center, you will be creeping ever closer to Tupelo, the birthplace of the king of rock-'n'-roll.

You will reach Old Town Overlook near Milepost 264. From this site, there are views of Old Town Creek and the surrounding flood plain.

Back in the nineteenth century, Americans would not try to learn the names of Indian villages on the Natchez Trace. They named one Chickasaw village Old Town and dubbed the creek running through the valley Old Town as well. This stream is one of the tributaries of the River of the Chickasaw, otherwise known as the Tombigbee. It was in this area that the fierce Chickasaw Indians defeated the Creeks in a battle that took place in 1795. An exhibit at the overlook displays Andrew Jackson's words to the Chickasaw tribe after the battle: "When the whole Creek nation came to destroy your town . . . a few hundred Chickasaw aided by a few whites chased them back to their nation, killing the best of their warriors, and covering the rest with shame."

This region was formerly the hub of Chickasaw Indian country.

Near Milepost 262, you will come to Chickasaw Village. Here, an exhibit shelter offers taped presentations that describe what Chickasaw life was like in the 1700s. Visitors can walk among the foundations of Chickasaw homes, both the rectangular summer homes and the sturdier, circular winter homes. There is also a loop trail leading visitors on a fifteen-minute walk past plants and vegetation used by the Indians.

If you wish to visit Tupelo, exit the parkway onto MS 6 near Milepost 260. A description of Tupelo's restaurants, accommodations, and attractions follows in the next chapter.

Campground

NATCHEZ TRACE PARKWAY

Tishomingo State Park
P.O. Box 880
Tishomingo, MS 38873
(601) 438-6914

This campground is located at Milepost 302.8 on the parkway. Among its amenities are sixty-two campsites for tent camping, a group camping area that can accommodate up to 142 people, six cabins, a pool, a thirteen-mile nature trail, and a swinging bridge. The park also offers a float trip down Bear Creek from April to October.

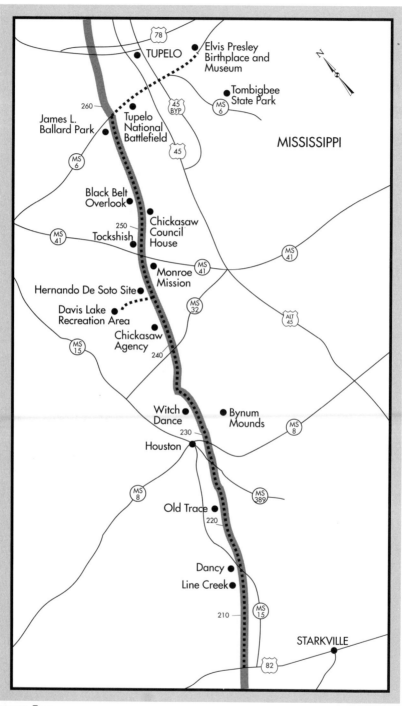

78

TUPELO

Elvis Presley
Birthplace and
Museum

MS
6

Tombigbee
State Park

260

45
BYP

James L.
Ballard Park

Tupelo
National
Battlefield

MISSISSIPPI

45

MS
6

Black Belt
Overlook

250

MS
41

Tockshish

Chickasaw
Council
House

MS
41

MS
41

Monroe
Mission

Hernando De Soto Site

MS
32

Davis Lake
Recreation Area

ALT
45

Chickasaw
Agency

MS
15

240

Witch
Dance

Bynum
Mounds

MS
8

230

Houston

MS
8

MS
389

Old Trace

220

Dancy

Line Creek

MS
15

210

STARKVILLE

82

•••••• Tour
▬▬▬▬ Natchez Trace Parkway

DAVIS LAKE

TUPELO TO LINE CREEK

Milepost Guide

TOTAL MILEAGE
Approximately 73 miles
TOUR ENDPOINTS
This tour begins in Tupelo, Mississippi, and ends near Milepost 204 on the parkway.

259.7   HIGHWAY INTERSECTION
MS 6 intersects the parkway here, giving travelers access from Tupelo.

251.9   BLACK BELT OVERLOOK
This site offers a view of a once-vast prairie which derived its name from its rich, dark soil.

251.1   CHICKASAW COUNCIL HOUSE
Picnic tables are located at this site. In the 1820s, this was the capital of the Chickasaw nation.

249.6   TOCKSHISH
Picnic tables are located at this site, settled by John
McIntosh in 1770.

245.6   MONROE MISSION
Chickasaw Indians were once taught various trades at this
mission. Picnic tables are found here today.

243.3   HERNANDO DE SOTO SITE
An exhibit at this site synopsizes the life and discoveries of
the Spanish explorer.

243.1   DAVIS LAKE RECREATION AREA
Exit the parkway here if you wish to take a side trip to
Davis Lake. Managed by the United States Forest Service,
the lake offers summer camping and picnicking. A visit to
the lake adds about eight miles to this tour's total distance.

241.4   CHICKASAW AGENCY
The agency for the Chickasaw tribe was located here from
1802 to 1825. Picnic tables are available at the site today.

233.2   WITCH DANCE
Picnic tables, horse trails, and rest rooms are located here.

232.4   BYNUM MOUNDS
At this site, visitors can see Indian burial mounds believed to
have been built between 100 B.C. and 200 A.D. Exhibits
provide information on the life of the Indians who
built them.

221.4   OLD TRACE
A section of the original Natchez Trace crosses the
parkway at this milepost. Picnic tables are located here.

214.5   DANCY RANGER STATION

213.3 LINE CREEK
This site marks the old boundary between the Choctaw and Chickasaw tribes.

203.8 HIGHWAY INTERSECTION
U.S. 82 intersects the parkway here and leads east toward Starkville, from which U.S. 45 Alternate gives access to Brooksville.

The tour begins in Tupelo, located adjacent to the parkway via MS 6.

Back in 1934, Vernon Presley borrowed $180 to pay for the materials to build a two-room shotgun house. On January 8, 1935, Elvis Presley and his twin brother, who died at birth, were born in this tiny frame home in Tupelo.

To reach the Elvis Presley Birthplace and Museum, drive east on MS 6 (Main Street) approximately two miles from the intersection with Gloster Street in downtown Tupelo. Turn left onto Elvis Presley Boulevard. The house and museum are on the right after 0.2 mile.

Elvis Presley's birthplace

Elvis and his family didn't live in this small house for long; it was repossessed by the time he was three years old. Standing in front of the humble white house today, you will find it a stark contrast to the opulent, glitter-and-glitz life Elvis knew in his later years as a movie star and the king of rock-'n'-roll. They say the legend still lives in Tupelo, and judging from the thousands of visitors to Elvis's birthplace, it must be true.

In addition to the home, you may also visit the Elvis Presley Museum, which includes a "Times and Things Remembered" exhibit. This showcase displays a collection of unique Elvis memorabilia. Janelle McComb, close friend to Elvis for many years, donated personal belongings, articles of clothing, and photographs which had been hidden away for years. You will also have a chance to read poems written by Janelle for Elvis's daughter, Lisa Marie. One exhibit recalls a time when Elvis was so emotionally touched by a poem written by Janelle for the occasion of Lisa Marie's birthday that he lost his composure and broke into tears when reading it.

Tupelo is also home to Tupelo National Battlefield. To reach this site, return to MS 6 (Main Street) and drive 3.3 miles west; the battlefield is on the left.

Not nearly as large as the battlefield sites in Shiloh and Vicksburg, Tupelo National Battlefield is similar to the site at Brices Cross Roads. It features monuments that pay tribute to both the Confederate and Union troops who fought at the Battle of Tupelo on July 14, 1864.

After hearing that General Nathan Bedford Forrest's men had soundly pushed the Union troops back at Brices Cross Roads, General William T. Sherman was incensed. In a letter to Secretary of War Edwin Stanton, Sherman wrote, "I have two officers at Memphis that will fight all of the time. I will order them to go out and make up a force and follow Forrest to his death, even if it cost 100,000 lives and breaks the treasury. There will never be peace in Tennessee until Forrest is dead."

Forrest and his men were still under orders from Lieutenant General Stephen D. Lee to destroy the railroad line running from Nashville to Chattanooga. The plan was to slow or stop Sherman's campaign against Atlanta by cutting him off from vital supplies. In an effort to thwart the Confederate plans, Sherman ordered Major

General Andrew Smith and Brigadier General James Mower to find Forrest and kill him.

Smith moved his fourteen thousand troops from Memphis into northern Mississippi by July 5, 1864. They were on their way toward Tupelo in cautious and calculated pursuit of "that devil Forrest." However, Forrest was waiting for Smith in Okolona, twenty miles south of Tupelo. Rather than aggressively advancing on Smith and his army, Forrest and Lee decided to form defensive lines and sit tight until Smith arrived.

But they didn't count on Smith's being sidetracked by the undefended Mobile and Ohio Railroad, a vital Confederate supply and communication line. Though Smith's primary objective was to kill Forrest, he elected to first move into Tupelo to destroy as much of the railroad as possible. He knew it would not be long before Confederate forces arrived. Forrest would now come to him. After dismantling sections of the railroad, most of the Union troops arrived in Tupelo. They quickly went to work preparing a defensive line in preparation for the Rebs that were on their way.

At dawn on July 14, the Confederates launched their first attack on the Federal lines. However, the attack was poorly orchestrated and executed. The Confederate troops so successful at Brices Cross Roads were now unable to penetrate Federal defenses. They were quickly pushed back. By early afternoon, the gunfire ceased. But Forrest wasn't quite finished.

The calm, peaceful sound of crickets chirping in the moonlight was abruptly snuffed out by the roaring report of muskets during the middle of the night. Forrest had mounted a starlight attack on the Union forces, hoping to catch them by surprise. The attack was unsuccessful. Though Smith did not succeed in killing Forrest, the Federal forces were the victors of the Battle of Tupelo.

Forrest survived the Civil War despite being wounded four times. A brilliant and feared officer, he was known for winning battles despite long odds. He was a thorn in the side of the Federals, particularly Sherman, as he unrelentingly harassed the Union supply lines along the path to Atlanta.

His spirited nature occasionally angered more than just his enemies. Once, after reprimanding a subordinate officer, Forrest was shot at point-blank range by the infuriated man. Though the wound was nearly fatal, Forrest grabbed his assailant with one hand and a penknife with the other and picked the blade open with his teeth. Stabbing the officer in the belly, Forrest glared at him and muttered, "No damned man kills me and lives." The man loosened himself from Forrest's grip and wobbled away, only to collapse and die. Forrest, however, was back in action in less than two weeks.

One last stop in Tupelo before continuing your tour of the Natchez Trace Parkway should be the Tupelo Museum, located at James L. Ballard Park. From Tupelo National Battlefield, continue west on MS 6. After 1.2 miles, you will pass the access to the parkway. It is another 0.4 mile on MS 6 to James L. Ballard Park, on the left. The museum is toward the rear of the park.

The Tupelo Museum is home to an amazingly diverse collection of items. From Indian artifacts to Elvis memorabilia to NASA lunar modules, the museum seems to have it all. Housed in old dairy barns, it is stuffed to the gills with thousands of antiques and other items. Civil War artifacts crowd one large section. Another is filled with antiquated medical instruments and equipment, including an iron

Tupelo Museum

lung. You will see a turn-of-the-century general store, complete with old mercantile items and a cash register. There is also an old beauty parlor with a barbaric-looking permanent-wave machine that may make your hair curl just looking at it.

After these dusty items from other eras, the space museum is a stark contrast. Several NASA space modules utilized on missions to the moon are found here, along with one of the first American flags to fly on the moon. There is also a spacesuit enclosed in a glass exhibit. And believe it or not, there's even a postage stamp that was canceled on the moon. Now, that's an exotic postmark!

You could easily spend hours browsing all the artifacts in the museum, but try not to tarry all day, because this tour offers much more when you return to the Natchez Trace Parkway. To reach the parkway, return to MS 6 and travel east for 0.4 mile to the access. Drive south on the parkway.

Black Belt Overlook, near Milepost 252, is the first site on this section of the Trace. Years ago, this region was actually under ocean water. The limestone found here was formed by years of shell and marine-life decomposition and settling. When the limestone was exposed to air and other elements through the ages, it gradually softened and was transformed into fertile soil. Predominantly black in color, the soil gave the area its name: Black Belt, or Black Prairie. Some also refer to this rich agricultural area as the Tombigbee Prairie.

An extensive region, the Black Belt extends south from here to below Columbus, Mississippi, and then sweeps across most of Alabama. In earlier days, the Black Belt was considered one of the greatest cotton-growing regions in the United States. Today, you may see a few token cotton fields, but the area is used mostly for grazing livestock.

The next stop is the Chickasaw Council House site, near Milepost 251.

About ten miles west of the Natchez Trace stood an Indian village called Pontitock, an Indian word meaning "cattail prairies." Pontitock became the capital of the mighty Chickasaw nation in the 1820s. Leaders and chiefs met in the council house to discuss tribal policies, establish laws, and sign treaties. Every summer, several thousand Chickasaws camped near the council house; they had sold land to the federal government during the year and were arriving to pick up their annual payments.

After the Treaty of Pontitock Creek was negotiated and executed by the Chickasaw Indians and the federal government in 1832, the Indians gave the government ownership of all their land. That treaty eventually rang the death knell of Pontitock. However, the name survived. The names of a county and town in Mississippi derive from it. The name has even been given to a county and town in Oklahoma, a reminder of the Indians' move along the Trail of Tears.

Just north of Milepost 249, you will arrive at a historic site called Tockshish. Back in the late 1770s, a village called McIntoshville stood near this site. It was dubbed Tockshish by the Chickasaws, a name meaning "tree root."

McIntoshville was named for a British agent, John McIntosh, sent to Mississippi to negotiate with the Indians. The town formed as Indians and whites began settling around McIntosh's farm. By the turn of the nineteenth century, the second post office established between Natchez and Nashville was located in McIntoshville. The village was also used as a "freshening station," or relay station, where post riders could rest, eat, and exchange exhausted horses for fresh animals.

The post rider's job was a grueling one. A rider leaving Nashville was expected to have mail delivered to Natchez, almost five hundred miles to the south, within ten to eleven days. The trip back to Nashville often took as long as three weeks.

Personal letters, newspapers, and government papers were delivered via post riders. In addition to the official cargo in his mailbags, a rider would carry a blanket, a bit of food, and a tin trumpet, which he used to announce his arrival. Whew! Talk about tough working conditions! It is doubtful that today's unions would put up with such labor practices for long.

Another Chickasaw site, Monroe Mission, is just ahead, near Milepost 246. The actual mission was located a short distance from this area.

During the early 1800s, many Chickasaws first learned about Christianity at Monroe Mission. Though one of the buildings at the mission was tiny—it measured less than sixteen feet square—more than 150 people were baptized in it at one time.

The mission was also used as a school. It was one of only three stations, or training centers, that educated future leaders of the

Chickasaw tribe. In 1827, there were more than eighty pupils on the roll. This was the Chickasaws' first encounter with formal education. In addition to traditional classroom work, girls were given instruction in weaving and spinning, while boys were taught farming and carpentry skills.

Speaking of schools, do you recall your elementary school days, when the names of explorers like Ponce de León and Christopher Columbus were drilled into your head? Does the name Hernando De Soto ring a bell? Ahead, near Milepost 244, is a historical site commemorating Hernando De Soto. This Spanish explorer spent a number of years in the Southeast in the early 1500s. De Soto was possibly the first European to travel a trail that later became became part of the Natchez Trace.

In 1540, he crossed the Tombigbee River somewhere east of this site and stayed through the winter. De Soto was in pursuit of gold and other treasures tucked away in these strange, new lands. He had little respect for the Indians, frequently ransacking the villages he stumbled upon. In the spring of 1541, Chicksaw warriors attacked De Soto and his army. Dozens of soldiers were killed, as were many more horses and pigs. Realizing that they had worn out their welcome, the Spaniards moved westward. During the summer of 1541, De Soto reached the mighty Mississippi River in northeastern Mississippi, south of Memphis. He is credited with the discovery of the river.

Approximately 0.2 mile south of the Hernando De Soto Site is the exit for Davis Lake Recreation Area. To take this side trip, exit the parkway and follow the signs toward Davis Lake. After driving 2.6 miles through open farmland, you will see Owl Creek Indian Mounds on the right. These mounds were built by people of the same culture that built Bear Creek Mound. There are steps that lead to the top of the mounds, if you wish to explore them further. It is another 1.4 miles to Davis Lake Recreation Area, which offers campsites with hookups, picnic areas, charcoal grills, and opportunities for water recreation. This area is located within Tombigbee National Forest and is managed by the United States Forest Service.

Back on the Natchez Trace Parkway, you will reach the Chickasaw Agency commemorative site a few tenths of a mile north of Milepost 241. United States government agents established an agency just west of this site and oversaw its operation from 1802 to 1825. The agents living here worked to ensure that Indians and travelers along the Trace got along harmoniously. These early peacekeepers had many duties, including employing the Indians to make goods, distributing annual annuities, collecting debts from white settlers, recovering stolen horses, seizing fugitives, and ousting tresspassers. The warm months were particularly busy times for the agents, as many boatmen journeyed along the Trace on their return trip home. Many travelers, including Indians, stopped off at the agency for a night of safe rest, as well as for a decent meal and medicine.

My children were mesmerized by the site near Milepost 233: Witch Dance. Reading the name of this site, even adults are likely to entertain images of coal-black skies, dark cats silhouetted by the faint light of campfires, and wicked witches dancing in a circle. You half-expect to hear their cackling cries piercing the quiet woods as they take flight on their magical brooms.

Local folks keep a legend alive that tells of witches that gathered here to dance. They say that wherever their black-slippered feet touched the ground, the grass curled up and died, never to return. You may find the hair standing on the back of your neck as you glance around and find bare spots of dirt.

There are rest rooms and picnic tables at this site—if you dare stay.

Approximately 0.5 mile south of Witch Dance are the Bynum Mounds. A village of Indians existed at this site more than two thousand years ago, during the Woodland Period. Known as the "Mound Builders," the Woodland Indians used these mounds as religious temples, ceremonial sites, and burial sites.

The Indians treated death as a sacred event, particularly when a chief or great warrior died. Bodies were buried with possessions, many of which were not indigenous to the central Mississippi region. In fact, archaeologists have discovered items buried deep in these mounds that suggest that the Woodland Indians had an extensive trade network. They excavated copper believed to have come from the region around Lake Superior, green rock from Tennessee, and flint from Ohio. The paths along the present course of the Natchez Trace were probably their south-to-north travel routes.

Exhibits at the site describe in detail the village life, farming practices, and hunting customs of these prehistoric Indians. You will also learn about the beautiful pottery archaeologists unearthed from the mounds.

Dennis Coelho

THE NATCHEZ TRACE PARKWAY AT MILEPOST 221.4

The last stop on this tour is Line Creek, near Milepost 213. During the days of the Chickasaw and Choctaw Indians, the concept of private ownership of land was foreign. Despite the fact that the two tribes were fierce enemies, they considered all land open and public. Property boundaries were rarely established by the tribes. However, this small creek was regarded as a dividing line between the two nations. The boundary remained in existence until both tribes were forced out of Mississippi to Oklahoma in 1832.

When you drive over Line Creek, bear in mind that two hundred years ago, you would have been leaving Chickasaw country and entering Choctaw territory.

If you wish to visit the towns of Starkville and Brooksville, exit the parkway onto U.S. 82 south of Milepost 204 and drive east. A few miles past Starkville, U.S. 45 Alternate leads south to Brooksville. A description of the restaurants, accommodations, and attractions in the Brooksville area is included in the following chapter.

Campgrounds

TUPELO

Tombigbee State Park
Route 2, Box 336E
Tupelo, MS 38801
(601) 842-7669

This state park is close to the Natchez Trace Parkway and only a few miles from downtown Tupelo. Twenty campsites are located here, as well as seven cabins, which can be reserved in advance. Campers searching for some exercise will enjoy the nature trail, the tennis court, and the archery range located at the park. There is also a lake on the grounds, where folks can swim or fish. Tombigbee's visitor center offers fast food, a game room, and other amenities.

TOMBIGBEE NATIONAL FOREST

Davis Lake Recreation Area
U.S. Forest Service, Tombigbee Ranger District
Route 1, Box 98A
Ackerman, MS 39735
(601) 285-3264

This recreation area is located less than four miles from Milepost 243.1 of the parkway. Davis Lake Recreation Area offers campsites with hookups, picnic areas, charcoal grills, and opportunities for water recreation. It is located within Tombigbee National Forest and is managed by the United States Forest Service.

Bed-and-Breakfast Inn

TUPELO

The Mockingbird Inn
305 North Gloster Street
Tupelo, MS 38801
(601) 841-0286

This inn, built around 1925, is located close to the Natchez Trace Parkway in the heart of Tupelo's downtown district. There are seven guest rooms to choose from, each with a private bath. Each room is furnished with decor representing a different region of the world. Different amenities are offered in different rooms: one has a fireplace, one has a Jacuzzi, one has a sitting room, and one has an outside ramp for handicapped guests.

Unique Dining

TUPELO

Gloster 205 Restaurant
205 North Gloster Street
Tupelo, MS 38801
(601) 842-7205

This upscale restaurant is open Monday through Saturday, serving lunch and dinner. Guests may choose from steaks, prime rib, seafood, sandwiches, and salads.

The Cottage Shop and Orleans Deli
208 North Spring Street
Tupelo, MS 38801
(601) 842-9191

For a delicious cup o' joe, this is the place. A variety of gourmet coffees is served to accompany the delicious breakfasts and lunches. Look elsewhere for a dinner spot, though, for this coffee house rolls up the welcome mat at five in the afternoon.

The Stables Restaurant
206 North Spring Street
Tupelo, MS 38801
(601) 791-0440

This restaurant serves breakfast on weekdays and is open until midnight Thursday through Saturday. Guests can choose from vegetable plates, "meat-and-three" plate lunches, seafood, steaks, and nightly specials.

Jefferson Place

823 Jefferson Street
Tupelo, MS 38801
(601) 844-8696

Serving hand-trimmed steaks as well as seafood and sandwiches, this restaurant is open for lunch and dinner Monday through Saturday. It is listed in Tupelo's restaurant guide under "Fun Dining," so plan to enjoy yourself.

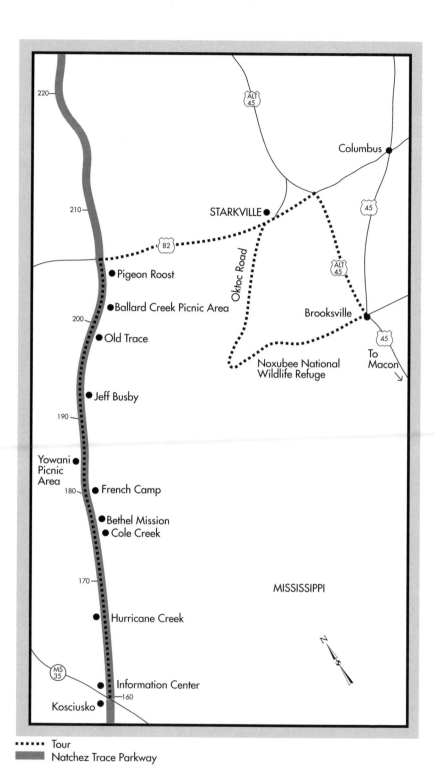

220

ALT 45

Columbus

210

STARKVILLE

45

82

Oktoc Road

ALT 45

Pigeon Roost

Ballard Creek Picnic Area

200

Brooksville

Old Trace

45

To Macon

Noxubee National
Wildlife Refuge

Jeff Busby

190

Yowani
Picnic
Area

French Camp

180

Bethel Mission

Cole Creek

170

MISSISSIPPI

Hurricane Creek

MS 35

Information Center

160

Kosciusko

N

•••••• Tour

Natchez Trace Parkway

TWO DOVES IN NOXUBEE NATIONAL WILDLIFE REFUGE

BROOKSVILLE TO HURRICANE CREEK

Milepost Guide

> TOTAL MILEAGE
> *Approximately 100 miles*
> TOUR ENDPOINTS
> *This tour begins in Brooksville, Mississippi, and ends at Milepost 160 on the parkway.*

203.8   HIGHWAY INTERSECTION
U.S. 82 intersects the parkway here, giving travelers access from Starkville and Brooksville.

203.5   PIGEON ROOST
Millions of passenger pigeons, now extinct, roosted at this site years ago.

201.3   BALLARD CREEK PICNIC AREA
Picnic tables are located at this site.

198.6   OLD TRACE

193.1   JEFF BUSBY
The only service station on the parkway is located here. A campground, a picnic area, a store, and rest rooms are also offered. For hiking enthusiasts, a nature trail located here takes about twenty minutes to walk.

184.8   YOWANI PICNIC AREA
Closed in winter, this site offers picnic tables during the warm months.

180.7   FRENCH CAMP
The historic buildings at this site can be toured. A bed-and-breakfast inn and a restaurant are also located at French Camp. Fuel is available nearby; service stations are located off the parkway on side roads.

176.3   BETHEL MISSION
Picnic tables are located at this site.

175.6   COLE CREEK
Here, a five-minute nature trail leads visitors through a cypress swamp.

164.3   HURRICANE CREEK
A nature trail which takes about fifteen minutes to walk is located here.

160.0   INFORMATION CENTER
MS 35 intersects the parkway here and leads a short distance to the town of Kosciusko.

The tour begins in Brooksville, reached by driving east off the parkway on U.S. 82 past the town of Starkville, then turning south on U.S. 45 Alternate.

If you are beginning this tour first thing in the morning, have I got a recommendation for a breakfast spot! Brooksville is home to one of the best bakeries in the South, the Olde Country Bakery. To reach the bakery, follow U.S. 45 Alternate to the junction with U.S. 45, then drive south on U.S. 45 for a few tenths of a mile. The bakery is on the right.

The food in this bakery is prepared by a group of Mennonites, who are some folks who really know how to cook. I have yet to eat at a Mennonite-run establishment whose offerings fell short of *incredible*.

My first experience with Mennonite cuisine was years ago on a thin-tire bicycle tour. Each year, my hometown bicycle club hosts a cross-state tour of South Carolina, usually drawing about seventy-five to one hundred Lycra-clad folks. On South Carolina's beautifully scenic backroads, we spin our way from the foothills down to the coast. Regardless of our beachfront destination, our first-day itinerary traditionally includes a lunch stop in the town of Abbeville.

Why Abbeville? Well, you see, there are two Mennonite-run restaurants in town that serve up delicious home-cooked food, sometimes called "Mama-cookin'." Whatever it's called, I have heard cyclists moaning after the first bite or two. It's that good.

So don't be surprised if the Olde Country Bakery in Brooksville becomes part of your tradition when traveling through this neck of the Mississippi woods. Once you've tasted the bakery's delicious food, you'll be hard-pressed to find another place for one hundred miles that can top it.

After loading up on the bakery's wonderful pastries, drive north on U.S. 45 and turn left before you reach the fork in the road. You will be driving down East Main Street, a charming country road of tall shade trees, well-kept houses, and proudly landscaped lawns. Birdhouses for the local population of martins sit high on stilts in side yards, and old-fashioned rope swings dangle from strong tree branches.

You are sure to find the scenery on this two-lane backroad quite pretty. My drive on a cloudless Sunday morning in early January was especially enjoyable. The preceding gloomy, gray day, complete with a steady winter rain, was replaced with stunningly blue skies and crisp, clean air. The countryside looked freshly scrubbed and sparkling from mother nature's bath the day before.

As I rounded a curve in the road, I saw an explosion of tiny birds taking flight from their cover of high grass next to the road. Slowing down to pan the woods for a glimpse of some wild critter among the swampy bayous and surrounding woods, I was not disappointed. A great blue heron lifted his heavy-looking body from a floating log and sailed slowly through the air before landing on a tree branch on the opposite side of the road. He tucked his great blue-gray wings close to his body, sat regally on his perch, and slowly turned his long, white head to the side, as though posing for a photograph. And who says Sunday drives are overrated?

After 9.6 miles on this beautiful backroad, the pavement suddenly ends. Don't panic, because you are entering Noxubee National Wildlife Refuge. The next few miles are on hard-packed dirt roads that are in excellent condition.

Turn right after driving two miles on the dirt road and follow the signs to the refuge office. There will be no mistaking the fact that you are traveling Mississippi backroads. The setting is gorgeous, the wildlife is rich, and the civilized world is blessedly far away. I stopped to speak to a deer hunter resting on the side of the road, who told me, "You're plumb on the other side of nowhere here!" I smiled at him. That was precisely where I wanted to be.

Approximately 2.7 miles from the turn, you will come to a stop sign. Turn left if you wish to visit the refuge office for maps or other information. If you enjoy mountain biking, these roads are perfect for knobby-tire pedaling. If you are interested in hiking, there are several single-track trails located here, including Beaver Dam Wildlife Trail and the Trail of the Big Trees.

But if you are ready to continue with the driving tour, bear right at the stop sign to head toward Starkville. You will immediately cross a bridge and see Bluff Lake on the left. A sign posted here says, "No feeding or disturbing alligators." Keep an eye out for these animals, particularly if you are on foot. White-tailed deer, wild turkey, feral hogs, and black bear also call this refuge home. But the birds may be the most spectacular refuge inhabitants of all. Winters are especially good for sighting birds, because of the increased population due to migration from the North. More than 250 bird species have been recorded at this forty-seven-thousand-acre refuge, including the endangered red-cockaded woodpecker.

You will come to a fork 0.3 mile from the stop sign; bear right to continue. After another 2.8 miles, you will reach an intersection; turn left. This dirt road almost immediately changes to pavement; you are on Oktoc Road.

Even though you will be zipping along at a faster pace once you reach pavement, the setting is still beautifully rural. Black-and-white grazing cattle are a striking contrast to the drab winter colors of the countryside. Huge flocks of birds cast dark, moving shadows across tawny, dried fields.

Gentry's General Store is one of the first signs of life you will see. This old country store is on the left after two miles on Oktoc Road. It has been around since 1932 and looks like it plans to stay around a while longer. As you would expect from a country store, just about any general mercantile item you want can be found inside its creaking, paint-chipped front door.

As you creep closer to Starkville, houses will begin springing up one by one. Soon, businesses will begin replacing the roadside woods. Approximately 8.9 miles from Gentry's General Store, you will reach a stop sign; bear left onto Spring Street. You will reach another stop sign after 0.2 mile. Continue straight; Mississippi State University's

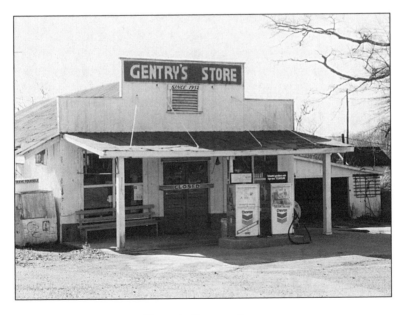

GENTRY'S GENERAL STORE

College of Veterinary Medicine is on the left. You are now in the city of Starkville.

Continue straight until you reach MS 12. Turn left and drive west on MS 12, then turn right onto Montgomery Road and drive 0.8 mile to University Drive. If you wish to stop by the chamber of commerce for maps and information on this college town and its "kissing cousins" of Brooksville, Macon, and Artesia, turn here; the office is located at 322 University Drive. If not, continue another block on Montgomery to Martin Luther King, Jr., Drive. Turn left; the road becomes U.S. 82.

Though you won't have time to visit all the attractions in Starkville and its neighboring towns today, you may want to put them on your list for another time. One of the most popular stops in Starkville is Mississippi State University's widely acclaimed Enology Lab and Dairy Science Center, where visitors can see wine- and cheese-making demonstrations. Another popular attraction is the Old Jail Museum, located southeast of Starkville in Macon, Mississippi. Macon also lures visitors with its interesting craft and antique shops. For the young and young-at-heart, Sunshine Farms—located east of Brooksville, about an hour's drive from Starkville—is a wonderful place. The farm raises miniature horses, miniature sheep, goats, geese, ducks, chickens, and even peacocks. A visit to Sunshine Farms during the month of May offers a special treat, as the strawberry fields are loaded with delicious, ripe berries that you can pick yourself.

Strawberry fields will have to wait for another day, though, because we are heading back to the historic Natchez Trace Parkway. From U.S. 82 in downtown Starkville, it is 20.6 miles west to an intersection with the parkway near Milepost 204. Head south on the Trace to reach Pigeon Roost.

In the late 1700s, a fellow from the Northeast named Nathaniel Folsom established a trading post near here. He and his Choctaw bride had a son named David, who later joined his father in the operation of this stand. As David matured, his interests extended beyond the trading business. Much of his time went to spreading the gospel and promoting the education of Indians. David became so admired by the Choctaw nation that even though he was of mixed blood, he was elected chief of the Choctaws' northeastern district in the early 1800s.

The name of the historic site where the Folsoms' stand was located is Pigeon Roost. The name was derived from the millions of passenger pigeons that migrated through this area nearly two hundred years ago. During the migration, they would stop in the forests near here to roost. There were so many birds that the tree branches would begin to sag and crack from the weight. Many of the branches eventually broke off. Even the oldest, strongest, and most massive trees suffered damage from the incredible number of pigeons. Alexander Wilson, the renowned ornithologist, was intrigued by the prodigious number of pigeons in this area. On one occasion, he observed a flock that, in his estimation, stretched for more than two hundred miles. That would have been several *billion* birds!

If you're starting to feel a little panicky as scenes from *The Birds* flash through your mind, or if you're just concerned about so many birds leaving their calling cards on your freshly washed windshield, worry not. Passenger pigeons are now extinct.

As you continue south, be sure to notice the vast number of dogwood trees sandwiched among tall evergreens. These small hardwoods are particularly plentiful along this section of the Trace. If you are traveling in the spring, you will find that the parkway looks like a charcoal-colored ribbon winding through a sea of delicate white blossoms.

After passing Ballard Creek Picnic Area near Milepost 201, you will arrive at an exhibit of the Old Trace near Milepost 199. Located here is a short preserved section of the original Natchez Trace that can be hiked.

At the beginning of the nineteenth century, many Americans feared that the Mississippi Valley settlements would form a separate nation because of their isolation from the rest of the country. In an effort to keep the settlements united with the rest of America, President Thomas Jefferson dispatched the army to clear out this old footpath and turn it into a crude road. The road was used by post riders to carry mail from the civilized world to the frontier settlements. Newspapers, letters, and government dispatches helped link the settlers to the rest of the United States.

Jefferson's post road was successful for years. It turned into a heavily trampled route used not only by post riders but also by boatmen, Indians, missionaries, hunters, traders, and others. However, when coal-powered steamboats emerged on the Mississippi River, a much more efficient method of mail delivery was born. The Trace was quickly forgotten as a post route.

Continue south on the parkway. Soon, you will arrive at Jeff Busby, located near Milepost 193. This site was named in honor of Congressman Thomas Jefferson Busby of Mississippi, whose work resulted in the preservation of the Natchez Trace.

In 1934, Busby introduced two bills in Congress. One requested funds for a survey of the Old Trace and the second sought funds for the subsequent construction of a paved national road. When debate on the bills was under way in Washington, Busby was asked why the Natchez Trace should receive national attention and government funds. After all, Congress argued, there were many other historic routes in America, such as the Santa Fe Trail, the Oregon Trail, and the Wilderness Road. Why should the Natchez Trace be singled out?

Busby's reply was probably very similar to President Jefferson's argument for establishing the post road along the Natchez Trace so many years earlier. He answered, "It is a utility proposition. A project of great usefulness. People of the country must find the best way they can from New Orleans, Baton Rouge, points in Texas, across to Nashville, Paducah, and other sections of the north and east, but there is no system of roads that is adequate to this particular territory and there is not likely to be any for many years to come."

Both bills were passed, and, to Busby's credit, the Natchez Trace was subsequently included in the national-park system. Today, the parkway hosts as many as 12.5 million visitors annually.

Jeff Busby is the only site on the Natchez Trace Parkway that offers fuel. A convenience store and telephone are also located here. The main road in the area leads to the campground and a picnic area. To reach the summit of Little Mountain, continue past the campground on this road.

At 603 feet, Little Mountain is one of the highest points along the Mississippi portion of the Trace. From the summit, you can see about twenty miles on a clear day. The trailhead for Little Mountain Trail is located on the edge of the parking lot at the summit. This 0.5-mile path descends into a valley filled with mature, shady trees. It doesn't take long to hike this easy path, but the scenery is quite beautiful. A wooden signpost near the convenience store maps out other short nature trails in this park, as well as the campground and the other facilities here.

If all the picnic tables are taken at Jeff Busby, continue south on the parkway to the Yowani Picnic Area. You will probably find fewer people here.

Keep your eyes open for white-tailed deer. I spotted a pretty doe very close to the Yowani Picnic Area one afternoon. She was standing stock-still, staring at my car, just as pretty as you please. As soon as I began backing up to try to get a photograph, her eyes widened in alarm and she quickly turned, showing me her white flag of a tail flying at high mast. She made her way to the edge of the woods and then stopped to look at me again. She must have felt safe within the cover of trees, because she didn't move again. However, her gaze never wavered from my direction. After several long minutes, I finally surrendered to this visual standoff and continued my drive south.

After leaving Yowani, you will soon come to historic French Camp, located near Milepost 181.

Louis LeFleur, a French Canadian, arrived in the area near present-day Jackson around the beginning of the nineteenth century. He lived and traded with the Choctaw Indians in a place along the Pearl River that later became known as LeFleur's Bluff. In 1812, LeFleur and his wife and children moved north along the Trace to this site and established a stand here. The area was subsequently named French Camp in honor of his origins.

Louis LeFleur's son, Greenwood, was a bright young man who showed great promise. Major James Donly, a post rider and influential Nashvillian, was impressed with young Greenwood and developed a keen paternal interest in him. Donly wanted to see that the boy got a proper education, so he took Greenwood back to Nashville with him, with the permission of his father.

Greenwood's French surname did not survive the Tennessee dialect. It was soon anglicized to Leflore, a spelling he kept for the rest of his life.

While in Tennessee, Greenwood got something else that he kept the rest of his life: a bride.

When he was seventeen years old, Greenwood fell in love with

Rosa Donly, the major's daughter. Though Major Donly thought the world of young Greenwood, he would not consent to their marriage, citing Rosa's young age of fifteen.

Not one to give up easily, Greenwood waited a few weeks and then changed his approach. "Major," he asked, "if you were in love with a girl and her parents objected to your marrying her, what would you do?"

Caught in a rare off-guard moment, the major answered, "Why, I should marry her first, and then tell her parents."

Well, I don't have to tell you what happened next.

Shortly after their marriage, the couple moved to Greenwood's home state, Mississippi. In 1830, Greenwood Leflore became the Choctaw nation's last elected district chief. That same year, he helped negotiate the Treaty of Dancing Rabbit Creek. This treaty required that the Choctaws leave the area within three years in exchange for land west of the Mississippi River. However, any Choctaw who agreed to comply with the government's laws could stay on the Choctaw land in Mississippi, and would be given 640 acres of land.

The treaty was finally executed after some shaky negotiations. For his diplomatic stance in helping to work out the terms of the treaty, Leflore was given twenty-five hundred acres of land. Thanks to that and subsequent real-estate acquisitions, he became an affluent plantation owner near present-day Greenwood, Mississippi.

Leflore continued his political career and was elected to the state senate in 1835. Today, a city and county in Mississippi are named in honor of this well-respected man.

The town of French Camp is home to French Camp Academy, a Christian boarding school established in 1885 for neglected and orphaned children. It has run without interruption since its inception. Today, the school offers Christian-based education for children with family problems. The beautiful one-thousand-acre campus is home to children from the seventh through twelfth grades.

A craft shop, museum, and gift shop are run by the academy; the proceeds are used to help fund the school. The gift shop is located in the Huffman Log Cabin, built in 1840 in the old "dogtrot" style. One-level cabins like this one were built throughout the American frontier. Today, only a few remain. The cabins had unenclosed central hallways running the length of the house, which frequently saw the traffic of dogs trotting through, hence the name.

FRENCH CAMP

At French Camp, you will have a chance to see Greenwood Leflore's horse-drawn carriage. He reportedly used this carriage on a number of occasions to journey to the nation's capital to meet with President Andrew Jackson.

Another historic point of interest at French Camp is the two-story antebellum home that once belonged to Colonel James Drane. Listed on the National Register of Historic Places, this house was built in 1846. Square nails were used in the ceiling and wooden pegs in the framework and foundation. Be sure to notice the beautiful mahogany mantels. Restored in Civil War-era colors, this house is owned and maintained by French Camp Academy.

If you are traveling in September, chances are good that you will get to see a demonstration of the molasses-making process. A working sorghum mill, which operates seasonally, is located on the property.

Council House Cafe and the French Camp Academy Bed-and-Breakfast Inn are also located here.

Continue south from French Camp. After passing Milepost 177, you will come to the site near where Bethel Mission once stood. Bethel, meaning "house of God," was the name given to one of the thirteen missions constructed by the Choctaw Indians. Bethel

Mission was built in 1822. According to an exhibit at the site, the men involved in its construction "labored hard during four weeks, frequently 'til 10:00 at night by the light of the moon or large fires, to clear the forests and erect the buildings."

Missionaries taught the gospel of Christ to Choctaw and mixed-blood children at Bethel Mission. Children were also taught the three R's, carpentry, farming, and weaving.

Only a few years after the mission was built, the Natchez Trace fell into disuse. Bethel Mission subsequently closed in 1826. Today, Bethel Mission Church is located near the site where the original mission once stood.

Less than a mile south of Bethel Mission, you will have a unique opportunity to hike one of the Deep South's enigmatic swamps. The short nature trail at Cole Creek leads through a beautiful swamp filled with water tupelo and bald cypress. These water-loving trees are prolific in bayous and swamps because of their ability to survive with their roots completely submerged in water. To help support the tupelo tree in its liquid environment, the base swells as the tree matures, forming the characteristic buttresses associated with classic swamp scenery. The bald cypress trees give the swamp another unique touch with their odd-looking knees. Though botanists once believed the knees were part of the trees' respiratory apparatus, they now believe that they help anchor the trees in their watery base.

Continue south to the last stop on this tour, Hurricane Creek, located near Milepost 164. Here, you will find a nature trail that offers a fifteen-minute hike. The path begins by threading through wet bottom land, then passes a medium-dry area, and then moves on to dry hilltops. The trail signs point out the different types of flora growing in each of these areas. You will see ferns and beech trees in the low-lying area of Hurricane Creek. As the trail continues up a hill, you will begin to encounter hickory trees, which require less water. By the time you reach the top of the hill, you will find that hardwoods and pine trees—which tolerate drier conditions, and even sandy soil—have overtaken the woods.

If you wish to visit the town of Kosciusko, exit the parkway onto MS 35 at Milepost 160. A description of Kosciusko's restaurants, accommodations, and attractions follows in the next chapter.

Campground

Jeff Busby Campground

Route 3, Box 80-A
Ackerman, MS 39735
(601) 387-4365

Located at Milepost 193.1, this parkway-managed campground offers eighteen campsites, a comfort station, a centrally located water supply, hiking trails, a service station, and a convenience store.

Bed-and-Breakfast Inns

STARKVILLE

Carpenter Place

1280 U.S. 25 South
Starkville, MS 39759
(601) 323-4669

Built in the 1830s, this house is the oldest in Oktibbeha County. Carpenter Place is a family home offering overnight accommodations to guests. There are two upstairs rooms with private baths. There is also a carriage house featuring two bedrooms and a sitting room. A full Southern breakfast is included in the price of lodging.

NATCHEZ TRACE PARKWAY

French Camp Academy Bed-and-Breakfast Inn

French Camp, MS 39745
(800) 377-2770 or (615) 285-2777

Built from several one-hundred-year-old log cabins, this rustic inn is located only two blocks from the parkway. A Southern breakfast of creamy grits, fresh eggs, crisp bacon, and hot biscuits and jelly is offered. Be sure to ask the hosts about the origin and history of this log cabin and its antique furnishings.

Unique Lodging

STARKVILLE

The Statehouse Hotel
P.O. Box 2002
Starkville, MS 39759
(800) 722-1903 or (601) 323-2000

Located on the corner of Main and Jackson streets, this small, elegant hotel is listed on the National Register of Historic Places. Evening entertainment is offered in the Library Lounge.

Unique Dining

BROOKSVILLE

Olde Country Bakery
U.S. 45 South
Brooksville, MS 39739
(601) 738-5795

Tricia Pace of Starkville emphatically told me, "This is the best bakery I have *ever* been to! One football weekend, we stopped by, and the place was mobbed with cars from all over; there was hardly a donut left."

The bakery is open Tuesday through Saturday from six in the morning until five in the afternoon. In addition to the breakfast sweets, you can buy sausage biscuits and ham-and-cheese biscuits. Po-boy sandwiches and soup are available from midday through the afternoon. You can take your goodies with you to eat on the run, or you can sit down for a leisurely bite at one of the tables.

STARKVILLE

Antoine's

P.O. Box 2002
Starkville, MS 39759
(800) 722-1903 or (601) 323-2000

Located in the historic Statehouse Hotel, Antoine's offers fine dining in an elegant setting. Guests can enjoy an after-dinner cup of coffee or glass of cognac in the Library Lounge, also located in the hotel.

NATCHEZ TRACE PARKWAY

Council House Cafe

(601) 547-6835

Located in historic French Camp at Milepost 180.7 on the parkway, this restaurant serves lunch on weekdays.

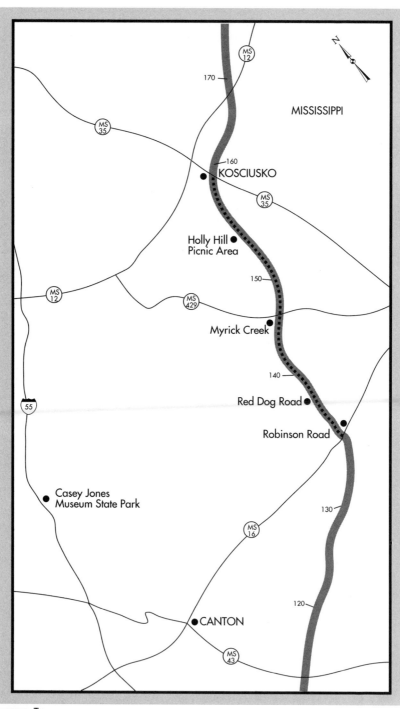

MS 12

170

MISSISSIPPI

MS 35

160
KOSCIUSKO

MS 35

Holly Hill
Picnic Area

150

MS 12

MS 429

Myrick Creek

140

55

Red Dog Road

Robinson Road

130

Casey Jones
Museum State Park

MS 16

120

CANTON

MS 43

...... Tour
▬▬▬ Natchez Trace Parkway

COTTON

KOSCIUSKO TO ROBINSON ROAD

TOTAL MILEAGE
Approximately 35 miles
TOUR ENDPOINTS
This tour begins in Kosciusko, Mississippi, and ends near Milepost 136 on the parkway.

Milepost Guide

160.0 INFORMATION CENTER
MS 35 intersects the parkway here, giving travelers access from the town of Kosciusko. A museum and rest rooms are located at the information center.

159.7 KOSCIUSKO RANGER STATION

154.3 HOLLY HILL PICNIC AREA
Rest rooms and picnic tables are located at this site.

145.1 MYRICK CREEK
A nature trail is located here. This stop is not recommended

for visitors with travel trailers, as there is no circular drive.

140.0   RED DOG ROAD

135.5   ROBINSON ROAD
MS 16 intersects the parkway here and leads south to the town of Canton. Interstate 55 then leads north toward Casey Jones Museum State Park, reached via Exit 133.

The tour begins in Kosciusko, located adjacent to the parkway via MS 35.

As you glance at the mad scramble of letters in the name, you may find yourself wondering how in the world it is pronounced. This Polish name has been Southernized by Mississippians. Around here, you will hear it pronounced *Kos-see-ess'-ko*. If you say it with a drawl and stretch out the last two syllables, you may be mistaken for a Kosciusko native.

Your first stop should be the Kosciusko Heritage Foundation Museum and Information Center, located within a stone's throw of the parkway. Here, you can find out everything you always wanted to know about Kosciusko but were afraid to ask. Descriptions of Kosciusko's history, namesake, attractions, lodgings, restaurants, and other services are all found here.

The town was named for Tadeusz Kosciuszko, pronounced *Koss-choos-ko*. The son of a Polish noble, Kosciuszko served under General George Washington during the Revolutionary War.

Kosciuszko was in Paris in 1776 when the streets pulsed with word of a possible revolution in Great Britain's North American colonies. He was wildly excited by the news. A military man with considerable experience, he had an unquenched thirst for military conflict and strategy.

As soon as he was able, Kosciuszko traveled to the colonies. He volunteered for military duty immediately upon arriving. Kosciuszko wasn't the only foreign officer willing to serve the revolutionary cause; many men from other countries volunteered for duty and were commissioned to serve in General Washington's army.

Kosciuszko quickly earned the respect of his officers with his engineering knowledge. He was a master fort builder, a talent that was critical to the defense of the colonies. It wasn't long before Kosciuszko assumed the rank of brigadier general.

During the final years of the American Revolution, Kosciuszko was stationed in the South, where he had an up-close look at slavery. He was so enraged by the practice that he made a provision in his will that set aside money for the purchase and liberation of slaves. Though his intentions were good, he made the mistake of asking Thomas Jefferson to carry out his final wish. A slave owner himself, Jefferson did not do so.

When the Revolutionary War finally ended in 1783, Kosciuszko returned to Poland and turned his attention to politics. Following in the footsteps of the colonists who challenged the laws of Great Britain, Kosciuszko encouraged his countrymen to demand the adoption of a new constitution. He then led them in an uprising against Prussia and Russia, during which he was captured in battle. After being held in a Russian prison camp for several years, he was released. However, his freedom was contingent upon a promise never to return to Poland, his beloved native country.

With a heavy heart, Kosciuszko traveled across the ocean to find a new home in America. Because of his heroic involvement in the American Revolution, he was greeted with open arms and treated like royalty wherever he went. American statesmen showered him with accolades. Thomas Jefferson described him as "the purist [*sic*] son of liberty." George Washington said that Kosciuszko "served America with courage and distinction."

Before this area was known as Kosciusko, it was called Red Bud Springs. The natural spring located here made the site a popular camping area for travelers making the arduous journey from Natchez to Nashville.

As the village of Red Bud Springs grew, the townspeople wanted a more distinguished name. They batted around a number of ideas before finally asking for help from William Dodd, a representative in the Mississippi legislature. Dodd's grandfather had served with Kosciuszko during the American Revolution, and Dodd remembered how his grandfather had spoken highly of him. Because of his grandfather's admiration for the man, Dodd requested that the legislature name the town in Kosciuszko's honor. Unwittingly, though, Dodd left out the *z*, creating the current spelling of the town's name.

Today, Kosciusko is nicknamed "Beehive of the Hills." No, the name has nothing to do with honeybees or out-of-fashion, harshly teased hairdos. It refers to the town's reputation as a bustling retail and industrial trade center.

This quaint Mississippi town has another claim to fame. A contemporary celebrity has close ties with Kosciusko. America's beloved daytime-television personality Oprah Winfrey was born in 1954 on a rural farm on the outskirts of town. She was actually named Orpah, after the Biblical Ruth's sister-in-law, but because of a spelling error—it seems that a pattern is beginning to emerge in this town— she became Oprah.

To reach Oprah's birthplace from the information center, drive north on MS 35 for 1.8 miles to Jefferson Street. Turn right onto Jefferson, drive 0.8 mile to MS 12 East, and turn right. After 1.1 miles,

Kosciusko

turn left on Oprah Winfrey Road at the signs for Oprah Winfrey's Birthplace. It is 0.9 mile to the modest home where Oprah was born.

Just past the sign for her birthplace, you will see Buffalo Community Church, where Oprah faced her first audience.

Return to the intersection of Jefferson Street and MS 35; drive straight across MS 35. Continue one mile on East Jefferson Street to Natchez Street and turn left. The Hammond-Routte House, located at 108 South Natchez Street, is 0.1 mile on the right, across from the library. The home is open to the public, with guided tours available Monday through Saturday.

This house was built on the original Natchez Trace next to a natural spring. Choctaw Indians, as well as Andrew Jackson and his soldiers, drank from this spring. Later, the spring water was used in one of the town's first businesses, the Kosciusko Ice and Coal Company, established in 1896 by William Jesse Taylor Hammond, the home's namesake and original owner.

The Hammond-Routte House is located just off the southeastern

HAMMOND-ROUTTE HOUSE

corner of Kosciusko's downtown Court Square, which is filled with a number of charming cafes, restaurants, antique shops, and gift shops.

If you are traveling through town in late April, check with the chamber of commerce for information on the Natchez Trace Festival. This is an extremely popular annual event that draws folks from hundreds of miles away.

To resume your travels on the Natchez Trace, return to MS 35 South and drive past the connector road beside the information center. Exit MS 35 on the right; you will be facing the Kosciusko Ranger District Office. Turn left on the parkway and head south toward Jackson.

You are now driving through a swampy region of Mississippi that is steeped in Native American history. Several miles east of here is an area that the Indians knew as Nanih Waiya, or "Hill of Origins." This was the Indians' promised land.

There are many conflicting stories surrounding the arrival of the Choctaw and Chickasaw Indians in this region. One often-repeated origin myth tells of a single tribe of Indians who traveled from the Land of the Setting Sun—the West—in search of Nanih Waiya. Two brothers, Choctaw and Chickasaw, led the tribe as they traveled many miles each day and set up camp each night. Every evening, they pulled out a stick that had been carefully packed away that morning. No, it wasn't used to bean the cook for burning the maize at dinner. Instead, it was used as a magical compass.

The Indians believed the stick had spiritual powers that would lead them to Nanih Waiya. Each night, the brothers placed the stick in the ground. Then, at sunrise, they checked it to see which way it leaned. Whichever direction it leaned—north, south, east, or west— was the direction the Indians traveled that day. They had faith that the stick would lead them to their promised land.

Not far from where this portion of the parkway runs today, the Indians came to a swollen stream and stopped. Choctaw wanted to set up camp and cross the creek the next day. Chickasaw disagreed and wanted to move on. Ignoring the objections of his brother, Choctaw grabbed the magical stick and thrust it deep into the ground. His brother turned away and crossed the stream to camp farther along. Nearly half of the Indians followed Chickasaw, leaving Choctaw and the rest of the tribe behind.

The next morning, Choctaw woke at dawn and immediately went to inspect the stick. It stood straight as an arrow. Anxious murmurs began rumbling through the tribe. What did this mean? Where would they travel if the stick offered no direction?

Choctaw held up his hand to quiet the tribe. Since the magical stick had not moved, it was a sign that they had arrived at the promised land. Choctaw told them it was time to rejoice. They had found Nanih Waiya.

Somewhere on the other side of the creek, Chickasaw and his group did not wait to see which direction the stick leaned; they broke camp early and departed. From that day on, the two bands remained separate and became bitter enemies. Despite the fact that they came from a single tribe and their leaders were brothers, they maintained a hatred for one another that was unparalleled in all of Indian history.

The first site on the parkway you will pass is Holly Hill Picnic Area. About nine miles later, near Milepost 145, you will reach the Myrick Creek site. If you are driving a camper or pulling a travel trailer, you should probably pass this site by, as there is no circular drive.

Here, visitors can take a ten-minute hike on a nature trail that snakes along Myrick Creek. An exhibit and signs along the trail chronicle the life of the beaver in these parts. Though beaver are no longer building dams on the creek, you will have a chance to see some abandoned dams.

You may think of beaver as being about the size of a house cat, weighing eight or nine pounds. However, some Mississippi beaver grow to "ninja rodent" size. It is not uncommon for Mississippi beaver to weigh a whopping fifty pounds. Sort of makes you wonder what's in the water.

Red Dog. No, it's not a new beer on the market. It's not even a Disney sequel to *Old Yeller*. Red Dog is the translation of Ofahoma, the name of a prominent Choctaw chief. Ofahoma was one of the Indians who executed the Treaty of Dancing Rabbit Creek in 1830, which forced the Indians to give up their homeland. You will pass the road named for Chief Ofahoma near Milepost 140. Red Dog Road was built in 1834; it ran to Canton, Mississippi.

One last point of interest on this tour is Robinson Road, located between Mileposts 136 and 135. Almost the entire length of this road ran through Choctaw country. Built in 1821, Robinson Road linked the Mississippi towns of Jackson and Columbus. It also intersected Andrew Jackson's "Military Road," which passed through Florence, Alabama, and on to Nashville, Tennessee. When Robinson Road was designated a mail route a year after it was built, much of the traffic on the northern part of the Trace fell off. The Natchez Trace no longer bore the distinction of being "the only direct road through the wilderness from the East to the Old Southwest," as an exhibit at this site tells.

If you wish to visit the town of Canton and Casey Jones Museum State Park, exit the parkway onto MS 16 and drive 18.2 miles west to the intersection with U.S. 43. Continue straight on MS 16 through Canton for 3.6 miles to Interstate 55, which leads north toward Casey Jones Museum State Park. A description of the area's attractions follows in the next chapter.

Bed-and-Breakfast Inn

KOSCIUSKO

Redbud Inn
121 North Wells Street
Kosciusko, MS 39090
(800) 377-2770 or (615) 285-2777

Featured in *Southern Living*, this two-story inn is one of Mississippi's finest examples of Queen Anne architecture. Built in 1884, it has a distinctive look, with its octagonal corner tower soaring three stories. The multicolored exterior is sure to catch your eye, as are the carved brackets, the balustrades, the spindles, the fish-scale shingles, and the turned posts. Inside, the wide central hall, characteristic of traditional Southern homes, is accented with heart-of-pine wainscoting. Be sure to notice the beautiful mantels fitted with tile pieces. The inn is located only two miles from the Natchez Trace Parkway and is ideal for travelers touring the historic path.

Unique Dining

KOSCIUSKO

Redbud Inn

121 North Wells Street
Kosciusko, MS 39090
(601) 289-5086

Owned and run by Rose Mary Burge and Maggie Garrett, the inn boasts a classic Southern tea room that is famous for the delicious lunches served on weekdays. Sometimes, Rose Mary has the help of her husband, Dr. John Burge, in the tea room. Dr. Burge is no slouch when it comes to serving customers. It seems that he had plenty of practice during dental school, when he waited tables to earn extra money. Though dinner is not offered during the week, it is served on Saturday evenings by reservation.

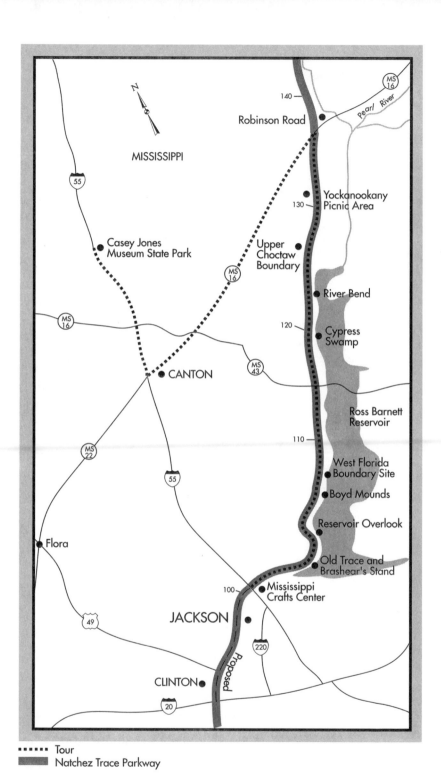

N

MISSISSIPPI

55

140

Robinson Road

MS 16

Pearl River

Casey Jones
Museum State Park

Yockanookany
Picnic Area

130

Upper
Choctaw
Boundary

MS 16

River Bend

120

Cypress
Swamp

MS 16

MS 43

CANTON

Ross Barnett
Reservoir

110

MS 22

West Florida
Boundary Site

55

Boyd Mounds

Reservoir Overlook

Flora

Old Trace and
Brashear's Stand

100

Mississippi
Crafts Center

49

JACKSON

220

Proposed

CLINTON

20

········ Tour
▬▬▬ Natchez Trace Parkway

MOSBY HOUSE

CASEY JONES MUSEUM STATE PARK TO MISSISSIPPI CRAFTS CENTER

TOTAL MILEAGE
Approximately 80 miles

TOUR ENDPOINTS
This tour begins at Casey Jones Museum State Park, and ends near Milepost 102 on the parkway.

Milepost Guide

135.5 ROBINSON ROAD
MS 16 intersects the parkway here, giving travelers access from Canton and Casey Jones Museum State Park.

130.9 YOCKANOOKANY PICNIC AREA

128.4 UPPER CHOCTAW BOUNDARY
A five- to ten-minute nature trail is located at this site.

122.6 RIVER BEND PICNIC AREA
Picnic shelter, charcoal grills, and rest rooms are available

at this site. Swimming here is not advised because of dangerous currents and deep water.

122.0 CYPRESS SWAMP
A twenty-minute nature trail is located at this site.

107.9 WEST FLORIDA BOUNDARY

106.9 BOYD MOUNDS

105.6 RESERVOIR OVERLOOK
For a nice view of the Ross Barnett Reservoir, pull over at this overlook.

104.5 BRASHEAR'S STAND

102.4 MISSISSIPPI CRAFTS CENTER
Demonstrations of Mississippi crafts and occasional hands-on programs are offered here. An arts-and-crafts gallery is located at this site, as are exhibits and rest rooms.

101.5 HIGHWAY INTERSECTION
Interstate 55 intersects the parkway here and leads a short distance into Jackson.

NOTE: At the time of this writing, the parkway was not completed from Milepost 101.5 to Milepost 87. Travelers are advised to use Interstate 55, Interstate 220, and Interstate 20 as connecting routes. Bicyclists should check with the Natchez Trace Parkway Headquarters and Visitor Center in Tupelo for route suggestions around Jackson, since bikes are prohibited on all interstates.

The tour begins at Casey Jones Museum State Park, accessed by taking MS 16 southwest off the parkway, then heading north for fourteen miles on Interstate 55. The park is reached via Exit 133 to Vaughan.

CASEY JONES MUSEUM

Turn right and drive 0.8 mile; the depot/museum is on the right at a ninety-degree turn in the road. A historical marker commemorating the exact spot where Casey Jones was killed is located after another 1.5 miles.

Casey Jones was a legend even before that fateful night aboard Engine No. 382. Ol' Casey had traveled so many miles through the Southern fields and hills that just about everybody knew him. He was a colorful character, tapping out a signature tune on his steam whistle that people instantly recognized and expected when he pulled his train into town.

On the evening of April 29, 1900, Casey pulled into Memphis aboard Engine No. 382. When asked to replace the ill engineer of the New Orleans Special—the "Cannonball"—Casey agreed to make the run to Canton, Mississippi. Sim Webb, Casey's fireman and right-hand man, agreed to go along with him.

With the Cannonball already well over an hour behind schedule, the men quickly hooked the cars up to Engine No. 382. Casey thought that with some serious speed and a little luck, he would make up the time and pull the Cannonball into Canton on schedule. But it was not to be.

At the Vaughan depot, two long trains had converged to be

rerouted. Knowing that the Cannonball was at full throttle and thundering down the tracks, the first of the long trains tried to move up a side track so that Engine No. 382 could pull the Cannonball past. However, as the train started down the side track, an air hose ruptured, which caused its brakes to lock. Three cars and the caboose were still out on the main track.

Though a flagman was sent up the tracks to warn Casey, the Cannonball was going too fast to stop. Hitting the brakes, Casey screamed for fireman Webb to jump. Casey was only able to slow the Cannonball to forty miles per hour before it crashed into the disabled cars remaining on the track.

No one in the passenger cars was killed. Fireman Webb was injured but survived. Casey Jones died at the scene.

Considered a folk hero for his sacrifice, Casey Jones lives on in legend. The story of that dark night was immortalized in the Wallace Saunders ballad "Casey Jones."

When you visit Casey Jones Museum State Park, you will hear the song played over and over inside the depot. The museum features railroad memorabilia, model trains, and exhibits. There is even a 1923 steam engine.

From Casey Jones Museum State Park, follow the signs to Interstate 55 and head south for approximately fourteen miles. Take Exit 119, turn left, and drive east on MS 22 (Peace Street) into Canton.

If you pick up one of Canton's promotional brochures, you might find yourself reading about old storefronts, artisans selling their crafts, and antebellum homes on quiet side streets. "Historic Canton is a year-round, storybook celebration of the tradition and culture of the Deep South," as one brochure puts it.

The best place to start is probably right in the heart of town at Canton Square, two miles from Interstate 55. This charming, historic downtown area is filled with dozens of turn-of-the-century buildings and shops. Many of these striking structures have been restored and are listed on the National Register of Historic Places.

The grand patriarch of Canton Square is the beautiful Greek Revival courthouse. This stately building is one of the oldest structures in the entire state of Mississippi. It sits in the center of the square with an appearance very much like a noble king gazing out across his kingdom. You will have a chance to stand in the courthouse's old courtyard—the very spot Confederate soldiers once gathered before marching off to war.

The galleries and specialty shops located in Canton Square will appeal to those of you who enjoy shopping. Here, you will find some real treasures made by local artisans. Canton is a hub for local and visiting artists because of its biannual Canton Flea Market. During this festival, the city greets thousands of artists and visitors from all over the country, who come to sell and purchase art, pottery, handcrafted toys, woven baskets, homespun fabrics, quilts, food, antiques, and other items. If you are traveling during May or October, you should definitely check with the Canton Convention and Visitors Bureau for details of this nationally acclaimed event.

Would you believe that little ol' Canton, Mississippi, is home to one of the premier art schools in the country? Well, it's true. The Allison's Wells School of Arts and Crafts is housed in a historic nineteenth-century building known as the Trolio Hotel, located on Union Street on Canton Square. The school is a rebirth of the historic Allison's Wells Resort and Art Colony, which operated from 1879 to 1963. It features a combination of contemporary teaching concepts and teaching ideas that were first introduced in the old art colony. Of the 347 arts-and-crafts schools worldwide, Allison's Wells was the first in the Deep South. It was also the nation's first such school to offer a formal artist/craftsman incubator center.

Classes and seminars are offered forty-seven weeks of the year. Students of all ages and skill levels may take a variety of classes. Quilting, basketry, weaving, calligraphy, sculpture, watercolor painting, and photography are just a few of the arts and crafts taught here. Visitors are welcome at Allison's Wells. If you go, be sure to stop by the school's galleries, where beautiful artwork is sold.

With the Canton Flea Market and the Allison's Wells School of Arts and Crafts, it is not surprising that Canton has been acclaimed "Mississippi's Premier Arts and Crafts Community."

Ready to leave Canton Square? A number of the town's historic homes and buildings are featured in tour packages provided by the Canton Convention and Visitors Bureau. We will visit three of the most popular sites.

From the Trolio Hotel on Union Street, turn right at the traffic signal onto Center Street and drive 0.5 mile. The large, white-columned Mosby House will be on your left at 261 East Center Street.

The striking Corinthian columns and cupola are sure to catch your eye when you reach this house. The grand size is also bound to make an impression on you. When the mansion was built around 1852, it was used as an in-town plantation home. The cupola in front was used to look out over the northern fields. With its opulent furnishings and several dozen rooms, the Mosby House was a prominent structure in Canton's early years. The center of many of the town's gala social affairs, it saw its share of beautiful belles in hoop skirts gliding down the grand, forty-foot-long halls.

You've seen where some of Canton's affluent citizens spent their days. Now comes the chance to see where the town's ne'er-do-wells were invited to spend some time.

The next stop is the Old Madison County Jail, located on East Fulton Street. From the Mosby House, continue driving 0.3 mile on Center Street, then turn right onto Madison Street. At the next stop sign, turn right onto Peace Street. Drive 1.5 miles to Liberty Street and turn left. After one block, turn left onto East Fulton Street. The Old Jail is on the right after 0.2 mile.

Built about five years after the Civil War, the Old Jail held many prisoners during its ninety years of service. Today, this structure is listed on the National Register of Historic Places. Be sure to notice the red-brick jail in front of the cellblocks; it served as the jailer's quarters for many years.

The last stop before turning our attention to the Natchez Trace Parkway is one of Canton's greatest discoveries. The Little Log Cabin, located behind the Old Jail, was uncovered in 1984 when a rental house was demolished. Beneath the rubble, this small cabin, with its twelve-inch post-oak logs, was discovered. Historians believe that the Little Log Cabin was built sometime between 1820 and 1830. It was moved to its present location and restored by the Madison County Historical Society in 1985. Tours of the cabin are offered by appointment only. Contact the Canton Convention and Visitors Bureau for details.

From the Little Log Cabin, return to Peace Street, which becomes MS 16. Drive approximately twenty miles northeast to the intersection with the Natchez Trace Parkway. Head south from Milepost 135.5.

The first stop on the parkway is the Yockanookany Picnic Area, located on the right after Milepost 131. Nestled in a mature pine forest, this is a lovely picnic area. If you are looking for a spot to set up an alfresco lunch or snack, this is the place. However, there are no rest rooms or other facilities at Yockanookany.

Near this site, a fellow named William Doak established a tavern on the Trace around 1812. It was at this stand that Andrew Jackson, Chief Pushmataha of the Choctaws, and other leaders met in 1820 to discuss a possible treaty between the government and the Indians.

The United States wanted roughly one-third of the Choctaws' land, which would have been more than five million acres. In exchange for this chunk of real estate, the government offered to give the Indians an estimated thirteen million acres west of the Mississippi River.

However, the Choctaws weren't interested in handing over their homeland to the government. After weeks of haggling at Doak's Stand, Jackson finally lost control of his infamous red-headed temper and blew up at the Indian leaders. It was ultimatum time. Jackson told the Choctaws that they had two options. They could voluntarily surrender the third of their land the government wished to own, or they could be forced off their entire parcel and have nothing.

Realizing they had no choice, the Choctaw leaders reluctantly signed the Treaty of Doak's Stand. America's tragic removal of Indians from their homelands had begun. Little did the Choctaws know that only ten years later, in 1830, they and every other Indian tribe in the area would be forced to surrender all their land and move west.

The Treaty of Doak's Stand invited hordes of pioneers into the area to settle.

Two years after the treaty, the capital of Mississippi was moved permanently from Natchez to LeFleur's Bluff. Because of Andrew Jackson's negotiations, which resulted in the acquisition of this land, LeFleur's Bluff was eventually renamed Jackson.

Between Mileposts 130 and 129, you will come to a site called Upper Choctaw Boundary. Here, you will see a line of trees that marked one of the boundaries prescribed by the Treaty of Doak's Stand. You will also have a chance to take a ten-minute walk along a nature trail. This trail showcases the southern pine trees, explaining different types and their histories in the economic growth of the nation, their habitat, and their management as a crop.

Dennis Coello

CYPRESS SWAMP

TRAVELING THE NATCHEZ TRACE

Continue south from Upper Choctaw Boundary. You may notice that the land has an increasingly subtropical look as the Trace inches ever closer to Natchez. The spiked green fronds of saw palmettos are now beginning to mix with the softer understory of the woods. As you drive, you will notice pockets of swampland occasionally dotting the side of the parkway. Rising from the green film on the surface of these swampy waters are majestic bald cypress and water tupelo. Beards of Spanish moss hang from the gnarled limbs of many of these trees, enhancing this classic Deep South scenery. This "moss," which looks like gray-green tangles of unraveled knitting, is actually a bromeliad related to the pineapple, and is not a true moss at all.

South of Milepost 123 is River Bend, located on the banks of the Pearl River. Since 1812, the lower seventy-five miles of this river have been regarded as the boundary between Mississippi and Louisiana. As the name suggests, pearls were once found here, by a French explorer named Pierre LeMoyne Sieur de Iberville, who sailed into the mouth of this river back in 1698. You would be wise not to try your luck for such treasures; signs posted at River Bend read, "BEWARE—DEEP WATER, TREACHEROUS CURRENTS."

Cypress Swamp, one of the most interesting sites on the Natchez Trace Parkway, is coming up next, at Milepost 122. This beautiful swamp was formed years ago by a river channel that was abandoned when the Pearl River changed its course.

Cypress Swamp is laced with a meandering nature trail that takes about twenty minutes to hike. As you walk, you may find that the fecund, earthy aroma rising from these murky waters is one not easily forgotten. Neither are the sights. Surrounding you are ancient cypress trees, some of which are nearly as old as the Trace itself. Gazing at their massive, buttressed trunks, you may be struck with a feeling that we humans have but a tenuous hold on life compared with these grand old trees.

This wilderness sanctuary proved forbidding to boatmen and other early travelers on the Trace. It elicited fear in the toughest of men. This place is the subject of scores of legends and enigmatic tales. There are stories of the glowing red eyes of a nocturnal animal lurking in the tangled brush, the sudden splash of an unseen alligator heaving his huge body into the still swamp water, and the scream of a wildcat piercing a moonless night.

Though these stories of things that go bump in the night must have raised the hair on the back of the leathery necks of the tough ol' Kaintucks, they were only stories of animals doing what comes naturally. By the calming light of day, the swamp appeared as a storehouse of treasures, a place of beauty and tranquility. Though the swamp was challenging to cross and difficult to skirt, even the rough-edged boatmen must have been impressed with its beauty—its mirrored waters, its grand reaches of cypress, and its early mornings shrouded with billows of fog over the sluggish black water.

Today, you can safely enjoy the beauty of the swamp on the nature trail. The first section of the path consists of a boardwalk that spans the absolutely still waters. White rays of sunlight are filtered through the leaves of water tupelo, creating dancing coins of light on the water. If you look across the swamp, you may see turtles resting on floating logs. Winged creatures are also found here in great number, much to the delight of birders. The rich swamp waters hold a veritable smorgasbord for wading birds and shorebirds alike. Even the great blue heron, also known as "the great fisherman of the swamp," lives here. What a grand sight it is to see a heron take flight and swoop over the water to nab a fish for dinner.

And of course, what would a swamp be without alligators? There are even a few of these grinning reptiles in Cypress Swamp. So when you are crossing the boardwalk, pay close attention to the objects in the swamp that look like floating logs at first. They might just look back at you.

Though the swamp is a visual feast, the sound emanating from this patchwork of water and foliage is even more intriguing. Bird calls and occasional reptilian bellows rise in discordant chorus, while just below the boardwalk, turtles, bored with sunbathing on the logs, plop into the water for a swim, leaving a wavering wake.

After leaving the swamp, it's back to the parkway. Bright orange wildflowers grow in profusion along the shoulder of the road during the summer. The surrounding forest is a celebration of green during this time of the year, as the thick forest of deciduous trees is dressed in its leafy finest.

After passing Milepost 115, you will be treated to a terrific view of Ross Barnett Reservoir. This glistening waterway parallels the parkway on the left for the next eight or nine miles.

These surroundings are much different from the heavily wooded areas you have been traveling through. During warm weather, look for boats pulling tanned bodies on skis, fishermen with shoulders glazed a golden brown, and other sun- and water-worshipers. The reservoir is considered one of Mississippi's prime bass-fishing spots. The trophy-size fish pulled from these waters lure fishermen from all over the Southeast to try their luck. The lake can become pretty crowded during the summer, especially on weekends.

Ross Barnett Reservoir was formed by a three-mile-long earthen dam built on the Pearl River in the early 1960s. It was named in honor of the Mississippi governor who served during the period when the dam was constructed and the lake was formed. There are picnic areas, restaurants, a campground, marinas, and facilities for launching boats at different spots along the perimeter of the lake.

The region you are driving through once belonged to the French. In the late 1600s, France laid claim to this area after La Salle's Mississippi Valley explorations. It wasn't until the end of the French and Indian War in 1763 that it relinquished that claim.

After the war, in compliance with the Treaty of Paris, Great Britain gained control of the territory that stretched from the Appalachian Mountains to the Mississippi River, with the exception of New Orleans. England also acquired one of Spain's colonies, Spanish Florida, at the same time. By combining the two pieces of land, England formed British West Florida, which included the lower third of present-day Mississippi.

During the Revolutionary War, when England was preoccupied with the uprising in the colonies, Spain reoccupied Natchez and subsequently took over West Florida. The war ended when the Second Treaty of Paris was executed by England and the United States in 1783. This treaty recognized the United States' claim to West Florida, which extended south all the way to the thirty-first parallel, near Natchez. Spain disputed the boundary, contending that the line should be drawn at the thirty-second parallel, near the spot you are traveling on the Trace today. For several years, the two countries argued over rights to this hundred-mile-wide strip of land.

Finally, in 1795, Spain accepted the thirty-first parallel as the boundary, thus ending all European power in the Natchez Trace region.

Casey Jones Museum State Park to Mississippi Crafts Center

However, the varied influence of England, France, and Spain have left lasting marks on this area and its people.

Almost immediately after passing Milepost 108, you will come to the West Florida Boundary site. A park-service exhibit located here describes Spain's claim to land south of this line. Picnic tables are also offered here.

On one of my trips, I saw a bicyclist sprawled out on the grass sound asleep, soaking up the sun's rays like an old hound dog. He was exhausted after putting in many challenging miles on the parkway. Though the Trace hosts several million motorists annually, it is also an extremely popular cycling route. Keep a watchful eye out for cyclists, and please be courteous when passing them.

Boyd Mounds and the former site of Boyd Village are ahead, just south of Milepost 107. These burial mounds were built by Woodland Indians sometime between 800 A.D. and 1100 A.D. The one mound visible today is only five feet high but covers an area one hundred feet long. Pottery dating back to 700 A.D. has been unearthed by archaeologists here, along with the remains of some forty burials. Scientists have found evidence that the mound may actually be three separate mounds.

While at this site, you can listen to a three-minute-long recorded message that describes how the mounds were built. The message also details life in Boyd Village, which was established sometime around 500 A.D.

An overlook of the Ross Barnett Reservoir is on the left about halfway between Mileposts 106 and 105. From this site, you will have an impressive view of this fifty-square-mile lake. The overlook is open from sunrise until ten at night. If you have a camera, this is a good spot for shooting a photograph or two.

South of Milepost 105, you will arrive at the site where Brashear's Stand stood in the early 1800s. This stand was billed as "a house of entertainment in the wilderness." I'll refrain from commenting on that advertisement.

A loop trail located at the site of Brashear's Stand leads hikers along a deeply eroded, sunken section of the original Natchez Trace. The loop takes only about five minutes to walk.

There are no picnic sites or rest rooms here.

The last stop on this tour is the Mississippi Crafts Center, located between Mileposts 103 and 102. Housed in an old "dogtrot" cabin, the center offers exhibits, information, and rest rooms. A combination gift shop and gallery located here sells a number of different items made by Choctaw Indians. You can choose from beautiful pottery, paintings, jewelry, quilts, baskets, Christmas ornaments, and other items. From March through October, weekend craft demonstrations and hands-on festivals are featured.

After leaving the Mississippi Crafts Center, continue driving south to Milepost 101.5. At the time of this writing, the parkway was not completed from this milepost to Milepost 87. You will see a barricade ahead; exit the parkway onto Interstate 55 South to detour the incomplete section of the parkway.

Interstate 55 leads into Jackson. A description of the city's restaurants, accommodations, and attractions follows in the next chapter.

Bed-and-Breakfast Inn

MADISON

Kirkhaven Bed-and-Breakfast
P.O. Box 69 Dogwood Lane
Madison, MS 39130
(800) 377-2770 or (615) 285-2777

This elegant home is located near Madison, Mississippi, which is north of Jackson. Since the inn is only six miles from the Trace, it is ideal for parkway travelers. Ten-foot ceilings help give the inn's interior a spacious feel. The heart-of-pine floors are adorned with beautiful Oriental carpets. All rooms have private baths. A two-bedroom suite is also available.

CANTON

Trolio Hotel
347 North Union Street
Canton, MS 39046
(800) 489-2787 or (601) 859-5821

Housing the Allison's Wells School of Arts and Crafts, this turn-of-the-century structure has forty-two rooms for overnight guests. A father-and-son team, Peter and Vic Trolio, opened the hotel in 1891. Though well known for its luxurious amenities, the hotel became even more famous for its bar.

A number of interesting newspaper accounts from the late 1800s and early 1900s chronicle the early days of the Trolio Hotel. An article describing the bar in the September 25, 1891, issue of the *Canton Picket* reads, "The barroom had walnut woodwork and was 'beautifully fitted up and papered in exquisite colors.' The saloon contained 'huge mirrors' and 'corinthian pillars of walnut' which framed the entrance to a large adjacent pool room. Even the immense ice box was covered in walnut veneer and decorated with plate glass and diamond-shaped mirrors."

Vic Trolio, one of the most popular and successful businessmen in the city, began bottling whiskey and selling it at the Trolio Hotel. An article in the November 24, 1899, issue of the *Canton Times* reads, "In referring to his famous 'Trolio's Bourbon,' Trolio stated that it came 'highly recommended by the medical fraternity' and was 'free of fusil oils and other poisons, thereby acting as a safe and desirable stimulant and invigorator.'" An article in the same newspaper dated October 24, 1902, states, "Vic Trolio recommended his own 'Two Stamp Whiskey' for the 'sick room and the sideboard.'"

Though Trolio sold his whiskey and recommended it highly, he rarely drank any alcohol.

Unique Dining

CANTON

Perry's Restaurant
108 West Center Street
Canton, MS 39046
(601) 859-7182

The slogan at Perry's reads, "When you can't go to Mama's, come see us." For down-home "Mama-cookin'," this is definitely the place to go. Perry's is open seven days a week, serving buffet breakfasts, lunches, and suppers. Especially known for its delicious fried green tomatoes, Perry's also serves pork chops, fried chicken, barbecued ribs, turnip greens, and the like. Enjoy.

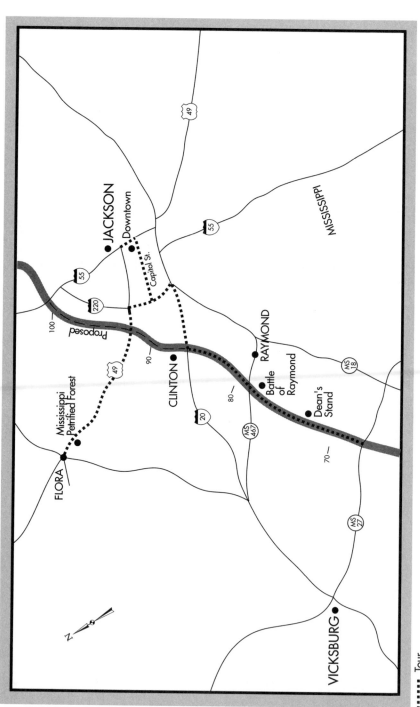

Tour
Natchez Trace Parkway

GOVERNOR'S MANSION

JACKSON TO DEAN'S STAND

TOTAL MILEAGE
Approximately 95 miles
TOUR ENDPOINTS
This tour begins in Jackson, Mississippi, and ends at Milepost 67 on the parkway.

Milepost Guide

87.0   HIGHWAY INTERSECTION
Interstate 20 intersects the parkway here, giving travelers access from Jackson. North of this milepost, the parkway is uncompleted to Milepost 101.5.

78.3   BATTLE OF RAYMOND
A Civil War battle was fought near this site in 1863.

73.5   DEAN'S STAND
Picnic tables are available at this site.

67.0   HIGHWAY INTERSECTION

MS 27 intersects the parkway here and leads northwest to Vicksburg.

Jackson, named for American patriot Andrew Jackson, is a city of richly varied attractions, both contemporary and historic. As Mississippi's state capital, the city is the hub of state government and the home of many of the state's senators and congressmen. Jackson has a bustling downtown area teeming with financial corporations, a world-acclaimed medical center, and top-name businesses.

Jackson is also a showcase for cultural activities, including performances of dance, opera, theater, jazz, and the blues. Every four years, the city is host to one of the most prestigious dance events in the world, the Olympic-style International Ballet Competition. Dancers from countries all over the world compete. A *New York Times* article on the event noted, "It was that mixture of unabashed graciousness and sophisticated theater that distinguished this competition." A visit to Jackson during this grand two-week dance event will give you an opportunity to see exemplary performances by rising ballet stars. That is, *if* you can land tickets.

It took many years for Jackson to evolve from the tiny village known as LeFleur's Bluff in the early 1800s to the thriving city it is today. The city later wore the dismal nickname "Chimneyville." That name was born after Union troops swept through the city in 1863 under General Sherman's orders to torch everything. The Federal troops left little in their smoldering wake. But the buildings that managed to survive have been lovingly restored, and many are open to visitors today.

As you drive from the parkway into the city on Interstate 55 South, the first attraction you will come to is the Jim Buck Ross Mississippi Agriculture and Forestry Museum/National Agricultural Aviation Museum. Now, that's a mouthful! Take Exit 98-B and turn left onto Lakeland Drive. Follow the signs to the Agriculture and Forestry Museum, which is on the left about 0.5 mile from the interstate. It is a sprawling complex of well-marked buildings and parking areas next to Smith-Wills Stadium; you can't miss it.

Straddling nearly forty acres, this complex of museums is quite impressive. The history of Mississippi's two most important industries—agriculture and forestry—is traced here. Inside the museum are exhibits that chronicle the history of Mississippi lumbermen and farmers, including such items as log wagons, experimental cotton pickers, presses, nineteenth-century cotton gins, and steel-wheeled tractors.

The cavernous National Agricultural Aviation Museum displays airplanes and other equipment used in the early days of crop-dusting.

Outside, a number of buildings from the Fortenberry-Parkman Farm are displayed. These authentic structures have been restored to depict rural farm life as it was nearly one hundred years ago. The first structure on this farm was a primitive storage shed built by Jesse Fortenberry, a squatter, during the 1850s. He hurriedly threw a few boards together to meet the government's requirements that he establish a residence within one month of occupation of the land. Jesse and his wife actually lived in this crude dwelling until they were able to construct a more permanent home. After Jesse died during the Civil War, his wife married a man named Jasper Parkman, hence the second part of the farm's name. Today, a smokehouse, a chicken coop, and other buildings stand in this living-history farm. Farm animals and costumed workers add to the authenticity of the display.

Near the farm is a replica of a small Mississippi crossroads town, complete with a general store, a doctor's office, a church, a sawmill, a filling station, and a two-room schoolhouse. Each of these authentic structures was moved from its original site to the crossroads town you see here today. The town is designed to show what village life was like in Mississippi shortly after World War I.

For you folks with a naturalistic slant, the Forest Study Trail is certain to be of interest. This short trail winds for less than 0.5 mile past trees and plants indigenous to this part of Mississippi. You will even have a chance to take an unsteady walk across a swinging bridge.

Before you leave, you may want to stop by the Arts and Crafts Gallery. This two-story log structure is a second home for many of the area's artisans. Demonstrations are given frequently by weavers, potters, and other artists. If you are interested in bringing home a piece of artwork, items can be purchased in the gift shop located next to the gallery.

When you have finished touring the Agriculture and Forestry

Museum, return to Interstate 55. Drive south to Exit 96-A and turn onto Pearl Street. After 0.2 mile, bear right at the fork to stay on Pearl. You will pass the chamber of commerce on the left at Central Station; it is located on the corner of Pearl and President streets. You may want to stop here to pick up maps and other information on Jackson's attractions. The chamber offers a leaflet describing a self-guided walking tour that highlights the sites in the downtown blocks.

Continue driving on Pearl Street to Lamar Street. Turn left on Lamar and drive one block to Pascagoula Street. You will see the Russell C. Davis Planetarium and the Mississippi Museum of Art straight ahead; both are located at 201 East Pascagoula. Park here to begin a walking tour of downtown Jackson.

The presentations at the Russell C. Davis Planetarium are fascinating for children and adults alike. You would expect to see shows about things cosmic and stellar—and you do—but there is much more to see than the stars. This facility ranks as the largest planetarium in the Southeast. It also houses one of the best theaters in the world. Many of the shows presented in the planetarium, produced with cameras equipped with unique fish-eye-type lenses, are known as Cinema-360. These shows offer viewers a wraparound effect. They can give you the sensation of being deep in the strong currents of the ocean blue, or of staring down at earth from a space shuttle, or of being surrounded by thousands of stars that dazzle a jet-black sky. The planetarium also offers NASA exhibits and exhibits about the solar system and the weather.

An extensive collection of artwork by American and European artists is located in the Mississippi Museum of Art. In fact, some twenty-five hundred works comprise the permanent collection housed here. On display are works by Georgia O'Keefe, Pablo Picasso, Paul Cezanne, and others. The works of Mississippi artists Marie Hull, Walter Anderson, and Theora Hamblett are also on exhibit.

For a hands-on experience, be sure to stop at the Impressions Gallery, located in the Mississippi Museum of Art. This four-thousand-square-foot teaching facility provides demonstrations on texture, composition, color, line, shape, and other art concepts. Children especially love this gallery. Where else can they make music by walking through beams of light? Or watch changing shapes in assorted mirrors? Or explore a process that enables two people to combine their faces? And parents, just when you were thinking that a surgical procedure was the only way to pry your child's sweet little hands from that Sega Genesis joystick, hang on. Help may be found right here in Jackson. Not many kids will pass up the chance to spend a few hours in the Impressions Gallery.

After leaving the Mississippi Museum of Art, return to Pascagoula Street and walk east for three blocks to President Street. Turn left to reach City Hall, located at 219 South President Street.

Serving as Jackson's city hall since it was built in 1846, this Greek Revival structure is one of the few survivors of the Civil War. The original building plan was changed when a third story was added, to be used as a Masonic meeting hall. This third-story addition may have been the key to city hall's survival during the war. Many say that General Sherman spared the building from fire because he was a Mason.

The building was used as a hospital and command post during the war. Though battered and bruised, city hall was still standing when the Rebs finally were forced to wave the white flag.

From President Street, walk north two blocks to East Capitol Street. Turn left and walk one block to Congress Street. Located on East Capitol between Congress and West streets is the Governor's Mansion, a stark contrast to the modern high-rise office buildings in the business district. Surrounding the mansion are beautiful, tall trees whose leafy canopy protects carefully tended flower gardens from the harsh rays of the sun. Dappled light dances across the well-manicured lawns.

Inside the mansion are rose- and gold-colored parlors, bedrooms, and sitting rooms filled with antiques. The furnishings are authentic to the 1840s, when the mansion was built. The Governor's Mansion has served as the official executive residence since it was constructed, except during the Civil War, when General Sherman seized it for command use. Not one to let such finery go to waste, Sherman reportedly hosted a victory dinner at the Governor's Mansion only days after the Confederate fall at Vicksburg in 1863.

This structure is the second-oldest governor's mansion in the United States. It is one of only two executive residences listed on the National Register of Historic Places. Designed by William Nichols, the mansion was built in the Greek Revival style. Tours are available.

After leaving the Governor's Mansion, walk east on East Capitol

Street two blocks to State Street. Straight ahead is the Old Capitol Museum, which sits at 100 South State Street on Capitol Green, the original downtown square designated on an 1822 map of Jackson as the site for the state capitol. When you open the museum's doors, you will be opening the doors to a storied past.

This Greek Revival building was completed in 1838 and served as the statehouse until 1903. Behind the closed doors of this building, many important men argued and finally signed their names to significant laws. In fact, the first piece of legislation to recognize the property rights of wives was enacted here back in 1839. Before the bill was introduced, the former law drew on English common law. But the new legislation was remarkably similar to the practices and customs held by the Indian nations.

Restored in 1961, the interior of the building is strikingly beautiful. Three-story spiral staircases curve from the ornate vestibule. High above the central reception room is a massive, iron-railed rotunda.

The Old Capitol now houses many historical documents and records. There are exhibits that chronicle the history of Mississippi, from De Soto's explorations to the civil rights movement to contemporary times. The Old Capitol Museum also displays memorabilia of famous Mississippian Jefferson Davis. There is even a poster dating back to 1865 which advertised a $100 reward for the capture of the president of the Confederacy.

Next door on the same block is the Mississippi War Memorial Building. Built in 1940 in the Art Deco style, the building itself is a unique attraction. However, its purpose as a monument honoring the Mississippi men and women who died while defending America overshadows the structure's architectural uniqueness. Exhibits chronicle United States military history from the Spanish-American War to the Vietnam War. On display are military uniforms, World War I posters, weapons, and even a scale model of the USS *Mississippi*, the third battleship named in honor of the state.

Behind the Old Capitol Museum, on Jefferson Street, is the Mississippi Museum of Natural Science. To reach the museum from State Street, turn right onto Amite Street, walk one block, and turn right onto Jefferson Street; you will see the museum on the right.

Inside, you will find more than a quarter of a million specimens of the fauna and flora that live and grow in the state of Mississippi.

Marine life that exists in farm ponds, hillside creeks, deep reservoir lakes, and the waters of the Gulf of Mexico are displayed in the museum's main aquariums. There are also dioramas that depict the natural environment of mammals, reptiles, and birds indigenous to the state's pine and hardwood forests, delta bayous, and barrier islands clinging to the edge of the Gulf.

The Eudora Welty Library sits at 300 North State Street, two blocks from Capitol Green. To reach the library from Jefferson Street, turn left onto Amite Street. Walk to State Street, then turn right. You will see the library on the right between Yazoo and Mississippi streets.

Named in honor of the city's beloved Pulitzer Prize–winning fiction writer, this is the largest public library in Mississippi. If you are not familiar with the work of this incredible lady, pick up a copy of *The Ponder Heart, One Writer's Beginnings, Delta Wedding*, or my personal favorite, *The Optimist's Daughter*. You'll be glad that you did.

Housed in the library is the Mississippi Writers' Room exhibit on Eudora Welty, Tennessee Williams, William Faulkner, and many others. If you visit the library, be sure to notice the forty-two-foot-long circulation desk. It was handcrafted by Fletcher Cox, a local craftsman, of curly maple and African rosewood.

You may want to return to your car now and drive to the remaining sites. Though a few more are located in the downtown area, they are more spread out than the ones already discussed.

From Pascagoula Street, turn onto West Street and drive north for several blocks to Hamilton Street. You will see the new Mississippi State Capitol on the right. Turn left onto Hamilton Street and drive to Bloom Street. The Smith-Robertson Museum and Cultural Center is on the right, at 528 Bloom Street.

Smith-Robertson Elementary School was built in 1894. What makes this school so noteworthy is that it was Jackson's first public school for blacks. Today, the school building serves as Mississippi's first museum devoted completely to the works of accomplished black Mississippians. Also, the heritage and roots of Mississippi blacks are depicted here through exhibits and displays.

From the Smith-Robertson Museum and Cultural Center, turn right onto Dr. Jesse Mosley Drive, which merges into High Street. Drive to Jefferson Street and turn left. The Oaks House is located

THE OAKS HOUSE

on the left after several blocks. Look for the white picket fence surrounding the house.

General William T. Sherman may have been Jackson's version of Goldilocks. It seems that any antebellum house or mansion that caught the Union general's eye was immediately seized for him to occupy, or at least try on for size. The Oaks House, the oldest house in Jackson, was no exception. During the siege of the city, Sherman occupied this antebellum cottage, built in 1853 by James Hervey Boyd.

Continue driving north on Jefferson Street, then turn west on Fortification Street. After several blocks, you will come upon the Manship House, a beautiful example of Gothic Revival residential architecture. The home sits between West and Congress streets; parking is on Congress Street.

During the siege of Jackson, Charles Henry Manship was mayor of the city. He was forced to surrender the town to the invading Federals but was able to live out the war years in this house with his wife and ten of his children. Yes, *ten* children. Actually, ol' Sherman may have tried to seize the house. The only problem was that musket fire and booming cannons couldn't be heard above the racket from so many kids.

At any rate, the house was occupied by four generations of Manships until the turn of the century.

The Gothic Revival style was unusual in the South, where most antebellum homes were built in the Greek Revival style. The Manship House's appearance is strikingly different from the other houses in this area.

The house has been restored to its mid-nineteenth-century appearance. The daily life of Mississippians during those years is depicted in exhibits of letters, photographs, diaries, and other items. There are also exhibits of Charles Manship's paintings and marbling. Prior to his political career, Manship was a professional artist.

If the weather cooperates, you may want to visit two outdoor attractions found in Jackson. One is Jackson Zoological Park, located at 2918 West Capitol Street. From the Manship House, return to Fortification Street and turn left. When you come to State Street, turn right. Drive to Pearl Street and turn right. After several miles, turn right onto Rose Street. Drive a few blocks and turn left onto Capitol Street. The zoo is on the right about 1.5 miles from the intersection of Capitol and Rose streets.

No spring chicken, Jackson Zoological Park has been around for quite a while. Built back in 1919, this zoo has one of the most outstanding collections of wild animals in the world. The latest addition to the park is the Discovery Zoo. Here, kids have a chance to learn about animals through hands-on experience and exercise. For example, they can clamber across a giant mock spider web or burst through human-size eggshells. There are so many attractions in this zoo that you may have a hard time getting a response from little Junior when you tell him it's time to go.

Continue driving west on Capitol Street from the zoo. You will reach Interstate 220 after 1.2 miles. Continue straight; you are now on Clinton Boulevard. Mynelle Gardens, Jackson's botanical wonderland, is located on the right at 4736 Clinton Boulevard.

As you stroll along the narrow paths winding through Mynelle Gardens, you will be enveloped by a modern-day Elysium. Open year-round, the beautifully landscaped gardens change with the season. Huge camellia bushes bloom during the winter, while aza-leas herald spring with splashes of brilliant pink, deep red, and pris-tine white. Day lilies sprout their yellow and orange heads after Me-morial Day, and annuals add to the vibrant show of color, blooming until the first frost.

Two houses on the property are used quite often for weddings and receptions. The sprawling green lawns outside the homes are perfect for outdoor ceremonies.

Visitors are invited to bring picnic baskets and enjoy a lunch on the grounds; artists and photographers are encouraged to paint or photograph the beautiful gardens.

If dipping back thousands of years into Indian history along the Trace has impressed you in previous chapters, then the next attrac-tion may boggle your mind. The small town of Flora, located about fifteen miles northwest of Jackson, is home to a petrified forest that dates back some thirty-six million years.

From Mynelle Gardens, return to Clinton Boulevard and drive to Interstate 220. Take Interstate 220 North for 2.5 miles to U.S. 49. Drive north on U.S. 49 toward Yazoo City to reach Flora. After 11.6 miles, turn left onto Petrified Forest Road to reach the Missis-sippi Petrified Forest. The forest is on the left after 1.5 miles. An easy walking trail winds through this forest of giant trees that long ago turned into stone.

Scientists believe that the petrification of this forest began when a catastrophic flood hit a huge swath of the earth. Entire forests from distant lands were uprooted and eventually landed here. This huge jumble of broken trees was soon covered by sand from nearby low-lying rivers. The minerals in the sand prevented the decay of the trees, which gradually turned to stone.

A walk through the forest today is a walk through a striking dis-play of history. These stone trees rest on the ground as silent left-overs from a prehistoric time.

In stark contrast to the ancient petrified pieces, a living forest has sprung up, dressing up the gray-colored rock with splashes of green. Late-afternoon visits add to the mystery of the forest, as long shad-ows are painted by the eternal silhouettes of stone.

The trail ends at a museum, where an impressive collection of min-

SCENERY ALONG THE PARKWAY

erals and petrified wood is displayed. You will also have a chance to see an assortment of fossils ranging from the outline of the tiny bones of a fish to the hoofprint of a dinosaur.

This petrified forest is the only one in the eastern United States. The National Park Service has declared it a National Natural Landmark. One of the few privately owned National Natural Landmarks, the forest is the property of the R. J. "Bob" Schabilion family. A picnic area and a campground are located here.

Though Flora is known primarily as the home of the petrified forest, it was also the birthplace of Belle Kearney, the first woman to be elected to the Mississippi State Senate. Belle was a leader in the women's suffrage movement and was a prominent activist during Prohibition.

When you are ready to leave this farming town of large, old homes and white picket fences, return to U.S. 49 and drive south to Interstate 220 in Jackson. (Once the section of the Natchez Trace Parkway through Jackson is completed, you will turn directly onto the Trace before reaching Interstate 220.) Drive 4.8 miles south on Interstate 220, then turn west on Interstate 20. Take Exit 34 off Interstate 20 to reach the Natchez Trace. Drive south on the parkway from Milepost 87.

The first point of interest you will reach is an exhibit near Milepost 78 describing the Battle of Raymond.

By the Civil War, the days of the Natchez Trace as a national road had ended. But a section running from Port Gibson to Jackson was still seeing considerable local use, though it veered from its original course through the town of Raymond.

In the spring of 1863, prior to the Battle at Vicksburg, General Ulysses S. Grant left his mark on this area. Grant led his troops across the Mississippi River to seize Port Gibson, then marched up the Natchez Trace before stopping near Raymond. A Confederate brigade commanded by Brigadier General John Gregg opened fire on the Federal troops. The fighting that day ended in another win for General Grant. The rebel boys retreated to Jackson, forced to leave their wounded in the county courthouse. The Battle at Raymond made Grant realize the importance of seizing the city of Jackson before the upcoming Union attack on Vicksburg.

The nearby town of Raymond offers historical sites for touring. The local chamber of commerce has prepared a driving guide to fourteen of the town's most popular tourist sites. If you are lucky enough to be passing through this area on the first Saturday in May, you may want to swing through town via MS 467 to take in the 1860s Country Fair. As with any decent, self-respecting fair, you will find singing and dancing, cotton candy and hot dogs, and handmade crafts for sale.

South of the exhibit on the Battle of Raymond, you will reach Dean's Stand, which commemorates the place where a pioneer named William Dean and his wife built an inn in 1823. Though the heyday of the Trace had already passed, the Deans took advantage of the Choctaw land that was opened up for white settlement after the 1820 signing of the Treaty of Doak's Stand. Farmers by trade, they supplemented their income with what they earned from travelers who lodged overnight in their inn. Among their overnight guests were post riders, missionaries, and traders.

Forty years after William Dean built this stand, General Ulysses S. Grant stayed here for a few days. After the Battle of Raymond, Grant established a temporary headquarters at Dean's Stand.

MS 27 intersects the parkway near Milepost 67 and leads approximately eighteen miles west to Vicksburg. Information on Vicksburg's restaurants, accommodations, and attractions follows in the next chapter.

Bed-and-Breakfast Inn

JACKSON

Millsaps-Buie House
628 North State Street
Jackson, MS 39202
(601) 352-0221

Conveniently located in the heart of downtown Jackson, the Millsaps-Buie House was built in 1888 by Major Reuben Webster Millsaps, who founded Millsaps College in Jackson. This Queen Anne–style home, with its columned porch and striking corner turret, is listed on the National Register of Historic Places. Each guest room is furnished individually with selected antiques. For breakfast, pastries and hot coffee are served in your choice of the Victorian dining room or the privacy of your own room.

Unique Lodging

JACKSON

The Edison Walthall Hotel

225 East Capitol Street
Jackson, MS 39201
(800) 932-6161 or (601) 948-6161

This comfortable hotel is located in the center of town close to the major attractions. Here, you will find all the amenities you expect of a good inn.

Unique Dining

JACKSON

400 East Capitol

400 East Capitol Street
Jackson, MS 39202
(601) 355-9671

This may be the city's best restaurant. *Nouvelle cuisine* is offered, as well as classic traditional preparations. However, if you are on a tight budget, you should probably choose another restaurant for dinner, because this is an expensive choice. Men must wear jackets and ties.

Hal and Mal's

200 South Commerce Street
Jackson, MS 39202
(601) 948-0888

For Cajun cooking or Gulf shrimp and other seafood, this is a good choice. The setting is relaxed and casual.

Iron Horse Grill and Bar

320 West Pearl Street
Jackson, MS 39202
(601) 355-8419

Tex-Mex cuisine deep in the heart of Dixie! Yup, the food served in this converted warehouse is prepared with a spicy Southwestern flair. Mesquite-grilled items are a favorite.

Elite Restaurant

141 East Capitol Street
Jackson, MS 39202
(601) 352-5606

When the local folk get a hankering for chicken-fried steak, this is the place where they head. Perhaps the most delicious homemade rolls in the city are served here. This is down-home Southern cooking, served in a casual atmosphere.

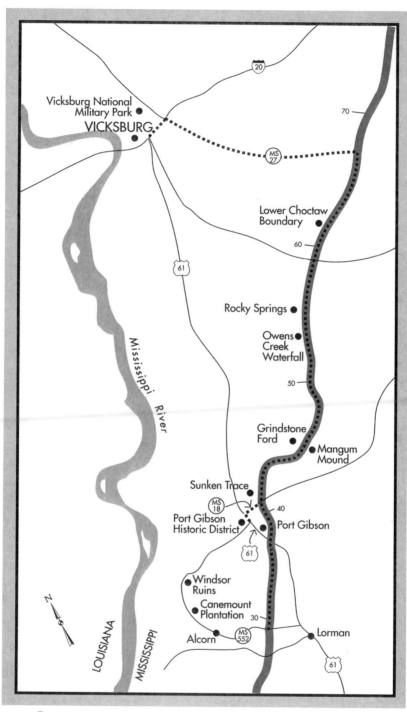

████ Tour
████ Natchez Trace Parkway

VICKSBURG NATIONAL
MILITARY PARK

VICKSBURG TO PORT GIBSON

Dennis Coelio

TOTAL MILEAGE
Approximately 70 miles
TOUR ENDPOINTS
*This tour begins in
Vicksburg, Mississippi, and
ends at Milepost 30 on the
parkway.*

Milepost Guide

67.0   HIGHWAY INTERSECTION
MS 27 intersects the parkway here, giving travelers access
from Vicksburg National Military Park and the city of
Vicksburg.

61.0   LOWER CHOCTAW BOUNDARY
This was once the dividing line between settled Mississippi
land and land belonging to the Choctaw nation.

54.8   ROCKY SPRINGS
This is the last major parkway-managed campground on

the Natchez Trace. In addition to camping facilities, the site offers picnic tables and rest rooms. A portion of the original Trace is available for hiking. A ranger station is also located at Rocky Springs.

52.4   OWENS CREEK WATERFALL
Picnic tables and hiking trails are available at this site.

45.7   GRINDSTONE FORD/MANGUM MOUND
A section of the original Trace, which can be hiked, is located here. There is also a historic cemetery at Grindstone Ford.

41.5   SUNKEN TRACE
A deeply eroded section of the original Trace is located here. It takes about five minutes to walk.

41.2   PORT GIBSON
You can reach the historic town of Port Gibson by exiting the parkway onto MS 18. Precise directions follow in the text.

39.2   PORT GIBSON RANGER STATION

30.0   HIGHWAY INTERSECTION
MS 552 intersects the parkway here and leads west to Canemount Plantation and Windsor Ruins and east to Lorman.

The tour begins at Vicksburg National Military Park, located west of the parkway via MS 27. The easiest way to access the park from the Natchez Trace is to follow MS 27 to a four-way stop at East Clay Street. Turn left on East Clay Street and drive a short distance to the park entrance, which is on the right.

Vicksburg. It is a name to be spoken with reverence. This historic city was one of the last major Confederate strongholds on the mighty Mississippi River. Here, the men in gray gave Union forces the fight of their lives.

The year was 1862. Pitted against one another were General Ulysses S. Grant of the Union and Lieutenant General John C. Pemberton of the Confederacy. Union naval forces had secured the city of Memphis, Tennessee, and from there, Grant was ordered to join Admiral David Farragut to secure the Mississippi River and divide the Confederacy in two.

Control of the river was of vital importance to the Union. If Confederate resistance could be removed from the river, the Union would enjoy undisturbed passage of troops and supplies into the South. The removal of Confederate defenses would also isolate Texas, Arkansas, most of Louisiana, and the Indian territory—nearly half of the Confederacy, and a region which supplied many recruits and important supplies.

From the beginning of the Civil War in 1861, Confederate troops established fortifications at strategic points along the river. And one by one, Union troops moved along the river and seized them. By late 1862, Vicksburg and Port Hudson were the last obstacles to complete Union domination of the Mississippi. And of the two, Vicksburg was by far the more important. Abraham Lincoln called Vicksburg "the key" and said that "the war can never be brought to a close until that key is in our pocket."

The city sat high on a bluff like a prized crown, overlooking a bend in the river. It was well defended by artillery batteries on the riverfront and by a natural defense of bayous and swamps to the north and south.

During the winter of 1862–63, Grant positioned his forty-five thousand troops across the Mississippi River from Vicksburg, at Milliken's Bend on the Louisiana side. Though he realized how difficult an attack from the opposite side of the river would be, he was afraid that if he moved his troops, his tactical plans would be questioned by the Union high command. So despite miserable living conditions—unrelenting rain, knee-deep mud, and sickness—Grant held his position.

Union morale deteriorated quickly. Grant attempted one amphibious operation after another, but each was repulsed by the rebel forces. Frequently called the Bayou Expeditions, all four of these Union attempts met with failure.

In the spring of 1863, with his troops still positioned at Milliken's

Bend, General Grant changed his strategy. He led his army south through Louisiana to a point called Hard Times. With the aid of Admiral David Porter, Grant planned to ferry his troops across the river from this point. The plan was to silence the guns at Grand Gulf and pave the way for a landing by Grant's troops. When the navy failed to silence all the guns, Grant searched for another crossing point.

The Yankees decided to move farther south before crossing the Mississippi. On April 30, they were able to cross at Bruinsburg, which offered no rebel opposition. Once on Mississippi land, Grant moved more than twenty-four thousand troops rapidly east. Near Port Gibson, they met up with some of Pemberton's rebel boys. These soldiers were a spunky group that gave the Yankees a run for their money, but they were ultimately overwhelmed.

Continuing on a northeasterly course, Grant's forces next had an encounter with Confederate forces on May 12 at the Battle of Raymond. The defenders were few; the Confederates were quickly defeated. From there, the Union troops stormed the state capital of Jackson on May 14. After a bloody battle, the Confederate defenders were again overwhelmed and defeated. Grant was on a roll.

Now, it was time to turn his army westward. It was on to Vicksburg. Following the route of the Southern Railroad of Mississippi, Grant encountered Pemberton's Confederate forces twice. The first fighting was at Champion Hill on May 16, when the bluecoats met a Pemberton-led group of almost twenty-two thousand men. The hill changed hands several times during the bloody battle before the Federal forces continued their westward march. A second clash took place the following day at Big Black River Bridge. Again, the Confederates couldn't hold back the concentrated Federals. The Yankees were hell-bent on reaching and seizing Vicksburg.

Grant, mistakenly assuming that the last two battles had deteriorated Confederate morale, launched an immediate attack on Vicksburg on May 19. But the Southerners had plenty of fight left in them and repulsed Grant's troops. He tried again on May 22 but was again turned back.

Grant realized that it was not going to be possible to take Vicksburg by storm. Rather than risk losing more men by continuing to attack, he began planning a formal siege. Admiral Porter's gunboats moved in and battered Vicksburg from the river. Grant's troops set up artillery batteries and blasted the Confederate forts from the land side. Vicksburg was now utterly cut off from the rest of the world. Though the Confederate forts were well prepared, the soldiers manning them were outnumbered by Union forces and were cut off from supplies and communications with the outside world.

The townspeople of Vicksburg scurried for cover on the local hillsides, richly endowed with loess bluffs. They dug caves into the bluffs, making ideal shelter against Federal fire. Many of the two thousand Vicksburg residents abandoned their homes and moved into the caves. Other, braver souls stayed in their homes but ran to the caves when the fighting got too close for comfort.

Mark Twain wrote the following about cave life during the siege: "Sometimes the caves were desperately crowded, always hot and close. Sometimes a cave had twenty or twenty-five people packed into it; no turning room for anybody; air so foul, sometimes, you couldn't have made a candle burn in it. A child was born in one of those caves one night. Think of that; why, it was like having it born in a trunk."

Ironically, the people of Vicksburg were reluctant rebels. When Mississippi took a vote on secession before the Civil War began, Vicksburg was opposed to it. But when the Yankees fired their first shot at the city, they quickly changed their minds, struggling to hold onto their city and the Mississippi River.

Vicksburg residents were a spunky lot. They viewed the Union siege as simply a frightening inconvenience that had to be endured. They took some furniture and a few belongings with them into the caves and tried to carry on as best they could for the next forty-seven days. The local newspaper, the *Daily Citizen*, even continued to be published during the struggle. When the newsprint ran out, the paper was printed on wallpaper donated to the cause. Diaries and journals written during the siege illustrate just how brave the townsfolk were. They show how the city's sense of humor prevailed, as guessing games were made up involving the size and type of shells screaming past the caves.

Somehow, church services continued during the ordeal. W. W. Lord, Jr., the son of one of Vicksburg's preachers during that time, wrote, "With the deep boom of cannon taking the place of organ notes and the shells of the besieging fleet bursting around the sacred edifice, [the pastor] preached the gospel of eternal peace to an assemblage of powder-grimmed and often blood-stained soldiery. . . . I have even heard him say, there never were more devout or attentive auditors."

Mark Twain, never at a loss for words, had this to say about the church services: "I've seen service stop a minute, and everybody sit quiet—no voice heard, pretty funerallike then—and all the more so on account of the awful bomb and crash going on outside and overhead; and pretty soon, when a body could be heard, service would go on again. Organs and church music mixed up with a bombardment is a powerful queer combination."

Days turned into weeks as an iron rain poured down on the city. The Federal forces had Vicksburg locked into a grip so tight that it was impossible to break. The Confederates were short of food, short of ammunition, and short of troops. They were short of everything but Yankees.

By the end of June, with no relief in sight, Pemberton finally conceded. Late in the day on July 3, he met with Grant to discuss terms of surrender. When Grant demanded an unconditional surrender, Pemberton vehemently refused. The meeting broke up with no resolution.

Later that day, Grant sent word to Pemberton that he was willing to make some concessions in the terms of surrender. He would agree to allow Confederate officers to keep their sidearms and horses. He also agreed to let Confederates sign paroles stating that they would not fight again until exchanged. Pemberton slept on it. Early the next morning—on the Fourth of July—he officially surrendered, just a day after the Confederate defeat at Gettysburg. It was a painful blow.

W. H. Tunnard, a Confederate defender at Vicksburg, wrote the following about the reaction of his fellow troops:

> The receipt of this order [of surrender] was the signal for a fearful outburst of anger and indignation. The members of the Third Louisiana Infantry expressed their feelings in curses loud and deep. Many broke their rifles against the trees, and scattered the ammunition over the ground where they had so long stood battling bravely and unflinchingly against overwhelming odds. In many instances the battle-worn flags were torn into shreds, and

TRAVELING THE NATCHEZ TRACE

178

Dennis Coello

EARLY MORNING IN VICKSBURG NATIONAL MILITARY PARK

distributed among the men as a precious and sacred memento that they were no party to the surrender.

. . . When the Federals first appeared . . . no word of exultation was uttered to irritate the feelings of the prisoners. On the contrary, every sentinel who came upon post brought haversacks filled with provisions, which he would give to some famished Southerner, with the remark, "Here, Reb, I know you are starved nearly to death."

That benevolence did not go unnoticed by the people of Vicksburg. In a highly unusual memorial, General Ulysses S. Grant was hon-

VICKSBURG NATIONAL MILITARY PARK

ored by the city's residents in 1885. The service took place at the Warren County Courthouse, which is now the Old Court House Museum. There are few accounts of *any* war that chronicle a general's being saluted by the people he defeated.

Vicksburg National Military Park was created to remember the siege and honor those who fought in the battle. More than one million people from all over the country visit this national park each year. A sixteen-mile drive winds through nearly two thousand acres of green, monument-filled land overlooking the Mississippi River. Imagine how this serene, rolling countryside looked in the summer of 1863. There were no carpet of grass, no fragrant, blooming magnolias, and no colorful sprigs of flowers. There were only blackened hillsides, splintered trees, and charred, barren spots of ground.

Tall bronze statues bear mute witness to the siege that gripped Vicksburg for forty-seven long days. All across this legendary battlefield are monuments to generals and soldiers—both Union and Confederate—that loom larger than life. As you walk among the ghostly trenches, you almost expect to hear the voice of a commanding officer shouting orders or to see a soldier on one knee cradling his dying buddy.

The park's visitor center has an impressive collection of books related to the Civil War. A museum displays artifacts from the siege, such as firearms, uniforms, personal items, and even a replica of a hillside cave used by the townspeople. While touring the museum, you will hear the boom of cannon fire rumbling overhead from unseen stereo speakers, a chilling reminder of the sounds heard in Vicksburg back in the summer of 1863. A film, *In Memory of Men*, is shown on the hour and half-hour throughout the day for those who wish to know more about the battle. Maps of the battlefield are available at the visitor center, as are rental cassette tapes that help guide visitors through the park from the comfort of their automobiles.

Don't kid yourself into thinking you can cover it all in a day. This is an extensive, impressive military park. It is estimated that it would take someone eight hours a day for three weeks to read every word on all the monuments and memorials.

Also featured in the park is the USS *Cairo*, moored in a dry dock overlooking the Yazoo River. Here, visitors learn the story of the first Union ironclad to be sunk by an electrically detonated mine.

A museum located next to the gunboat displays artifacts recovered from the *Cairo* after it was raised from the bottom of the Yazoo.

And finally, a curve of the road brings visitors to Vicksburg National Cemetery, where the majority of the seventeen thousand simple tombstones are marked only "Unknown." In each and every one of these graves rests the remains of some Union soldier. All the Confederate troops were buried, with less fanfare, in Vicksburg's city cemetery, which is outside the national park.

Though many tourists visit Vicksburg National Military Park and then move on, there are quite a few attractions in the city, if you have the luxury of time. As you move from the scene of battle to the quiet streets and cobblestone alleys, history continues to unfold. Come sit for a spell and listen to history's stories.

With so much to see and do in Vicksburg, your best bet is to stop by the Vicksburg Convention and Visitors Bureau after your tour of Vicksburg National Military Park. The bureau offers a free driving-tour map that highlights most of the city's historic attractions. The traffic signals are numbered, which greatly helps visitors as they navigate town. The tour is well marked with blue-and-white directional signs. If ever in doubt, follow the arrows.

After leaving the military park, turn right onto Clay Street. Drive to Traffic Signal 6 and turn right onto First North Street. Turn left at the first stop sign onto Grove Street, a red-brick road. The Martha Vick House is on the left at 1300 Grove Street.

Newit Vick, the town's founder, built this house around 1830 for his daughter, who never married. Today, this beautiful example of Greek Revival architecture is filled with period furnishings and French Impressionist paintings. Antique Haviland china and sparkling sterling silver adorn the dining-room table.

From the Martha Vick House, continue on Grove Street. Turn right onto Locust Street and drive down a hill to a stop sign. You will see the gorgeous Duff Green Mansion on the left. Turn left onto First East Street and proceed through a four-way stop. The mustard-colored Anchuca Inn is on the left. Be sure to notice the huge gas-burning lanterns that flicker faintly in the evening.

Continue on First East Street to the next stop sign; turn left onto Cherry Street. Take the first left onto Main Street. At the next intersection, you will see Lakemont House on the corner of Main and Adams streets.

The perfumed ghost of the mistress of Lakemont is rumored to appear on occasion. Legend has it that a servant raced into the house to tell the wife of Judge William Lake that her husband was engaged in a duel on De Soto Island, which is visible from the city. Spilling the perfume bottle she was holding, Mrs. Lake flew up the stairs, grabbed her opera glass, and watched in horror from the upstairs veranda as her husband was killed. According to the stories, the scent of her perfume still lingers in the house. Occasionally, her diaphanous figure is glimpsed floating down the stairs.

Turn right onto Adams and drive one block to Jackson Street. Turn right onto Jackson, then left onto Cherry Street. The Old Court House Museum is on the right. As I walked up to this museum on one of my visits to Vicksburg, I was lost in thought as I imagined the sounds of Union ships firing at this beautiful building. Then I was suddenly pulled back to the present by the sound of church bells tolling in the distance. It was the sound of peace ringing through a city that still remembers the sound of war.

Located on Court House Square, the Old Court House Museum, built around 1857, once served as the Warren County Courthouse. During the siege of Vicksburg, this distinctive landmark was a favorite target for Admiral David Farragut's gunboats. The Southerners weren't the least bit amused that the Yankees were toying with one of the most prominent structures in the city, so they turned the courthouse into a prison for captured Federals. The old courthouse never saw another round of fire.

This building is now a National Historic Landmark. The museum houses a wide collection of war memorabilia, including items that belonged to General Ulysses S. Grant, along with some amazing artifacts that date back to the early years of the city of Vicksburg. You will see a Ku Klux Klan hood, Indian artifacts, and much more on display here.

Continue down Cherry Street to Traffic Signal 3; turn right onto Clay Street. Drive to the end of Clay and you will see Harrah's Casino straight ahead, on the bank of the Yazoo River Diversion Canal. Turn right and follow the signs for the historic driving tour up a hill, then turn right onto Washington Street. Yesterday's Children Doll

Museum and Shop is on the right at 1104 Washington.

Yesterday's Children will appease any young people who have grown tired of Civil War relics. Little girls especially appreciate this fantasyland of thousands of dolls. There are my daughters' favorites—Madame Alexander dolls—as well as Barbies, porcelain dolls, and international dolls.

Across the street from Yesterday's Children is the Joseph Biedenharn Museum, known as the Biedenharn Candy Company, located at 1107 Washington.

Back in 1894, Joseph Biedenharn, an enterprising candy merchant, became the first man to bottle Coca-Cola and ship it to rural areas. Until then, it was only a soda-fountain beverage. In celebration of this enterprise, the museum bubbles with memorabilia such as bottles and posters bearing the famous logo.

The Corner Drug Store, also known as the Corner Medical Center, is located next door to the Joseph Biedenharn Museum.

An eclectic collection of artifacts, from antique firearms to apothecary items, is housed in the Corner Drug Store. The proprietor, J. A. Gerache, Sr., has collected a wide range of items. He even has lead bullets bearing the indentations of human teeth. There was such a shortage of supplies during the Vicksburg siege that field doctors had little more to offer wounded men than a bullet to bite on.

Many other historic mansions and buildings are found in Vicksburg—McRaven, Planters Hall, Buelow Home, and more. Also note that some of the bed-and-breakfast lodgings listed at the end of this chapter offer tours.

Now, though, it's time to turn our attention eastward, to the Natchez Trace Parkway. To reach the Trace from the Corner Drug Store, continue on Washington Street for several miles to Interstate 20. Turn onto Interstate 20 East and drive 4.1 miles to Exit 4A, East Clay Street. Drive 0.6 mile on East Clay to a four-way stop. Turn right onto MS 27 South and drive 16.7 miles to reach the parkway. You will return to the Trace near Milepost 67.

The first historic site on the parkway is Lower Choctaw Boundary, located at Milepost 61. For more than two hundred years, a line of trees at this site was regarded as the eastern boundary of the Old Natchez District. The line ran from a point twelve miles east of Vicksburg southward to the thirty-first parallel. The land east of this line belonged to England until 1777, then to Spain until 1792, and then to the United States beginning in 1801. The land west of the line belonged to the Choctaw nation until the 1820 signing of the Treaty of Doak's Stand.

The boundary line that once separated Choctaw land from white settlement now separates two Mississippi counties.

Located near this site was Red Bluff Stand, another stopping point for travelers on the Trace. Established in 1802, this stand was the last place a northbound traveler could pick up groceries. Owned and operated by John Gregg, Red Bluff Stand offered a large supply of provisions. Folks journeying the Trace could buy such items as ground coffee, sugar, cheese, biscuits, and dried meats. And, as a precursor of the modern service-station mechanic, Gregg would also shoe horses "on the shortest notice."

Continue south on the parkway. The next historic site is Rocky Springs, near Milepost 55. Now a ghost town, Rocky Springs was a thriving settlement in the early 1800s.

People began settling here in the 1790s, and the population grew to several thousand before the first shot of the Civil War was fired. In addition to private homes, Rocky Springs had a school, a post office, stores, a Masonic lodge, and a Methodist church.

The demise of the town began in May 1863, when General Ulysses S. Grant and his army of more than forty thousand men dropped in on Rocky Springs for a surprise visit. Establishing a Federal headquarters here, the Union troops stayed for several days. Their "invasion" of this small town was devastating.

Instead of the future brightening after the Civil War, fate dealt Rocky Springs another cruel blow. In 1878, a yellow-fever epidemic broke out. Many of the town's residents came down with the disease, and nearly fifty died from it. After the yellow-fever outbreak, the town seemed to be recovering slowly. Then another crisis hit in the early 1900s. Poor land management having already ravaged the soil, the town's agricultural mainstay—cotton—was devastated by the arrival of the boll weevil. This final disaster rang the death knell of the town. The land was barren, the water of the spring stopped flowing, and the few remaining residents finally left.

The only structure still standing today is the single-story, red-brick Methodist church, built in 1837. Church services are still held on a regular basis in this historic building. A small cemetery rests on a hilltop under tall trees draped with Spanish moss. Sitting forlornly in the weeds is a neglected, rusted cistern, a remnant of a blacksmith shop that once stood here. Two abandoned safes are about the only other traces of the once-bustling town.

A shady, pleasant trail winds through this ghost town, leading to the church and past the cistern and safe. Markers along the trail tell the story of Rocky Springs and point out areas of interest.

Also located at the Rocky Springs site is the last major campground on the Natchez Trace Parkway. No hookups are available, but tent pads, grills, and picnic tables are located at all campsites. There are also rest rooms, a ranger station, a picnic area, and a public telephone. An easy, short hiking trail follows part of the Old Trace through the low hills.

Continue south from Rocky Springs. The next stop is Owens Creek Waterfall, located between Mileposts 53 and 52. Here, you will find picnic tables and a 2.5-mile hiking trail that leads back to Rocky Springs.

If you're looking for waterfalls like those on the Niagara River, you'll have to travel to New York. Actually, there is not much of a waterfall here at all these days. However, many years ago, Owens Creek Waterfall was a familiar sight to boatmen and others journeying along the Trace. Before the water table dropped, it was fed by a freshwater spring. Now, the spring has dried up. Water still flows over this waterfall, but there is usually just a trickle of water unless heavy rains have fallen recently.

You will soon cross Bayou Pierre, one of Mississippi's many bayous. These swampy areas are actually the marshy inlets or outlets of a creek, lake, or river. The name comes from the Choctaw word *bayuk*, meaning "small stream."

Near Milepost 46 are two sites: Grindstone Ford and Mangum Mound.

To reach Grindstone Ford, exit to the right and drive about 0.5 mile to the ford. Named for a nearby mill, this ford was where most travelers chose to cross Bayou Pierre. Travelers coming from Natchez knew that once they crossed this ford, they were leaving the Old Natchez District, a relatively civilized area. From this point on, they would be journeying through the unknown wilderness of the Choctaw nation as they headed north.

During the Civil War, the bridge spanning Bayou Pierre at Grindstone Ford was burned by Confederates. They had been defeated at Port Gibson and were retreating from the Union troops, who were in hot pursuit. With the bridge gone, the bluecoats were at least slowed down, as they were forced to find another way to cross Bayou Pierre.

Mangum Site, the other exhibit near Milepost 46, is located on the east side of the parkway. You can reach it by exiting onto the road that passes under the parkway and driving about 0.5 mile.

Mangum Site was a pre-historic burial site used by Plaquemine Culture Indians centuries ago. Archaeologists have discovered an unusually large number of infant remains here. It is possible that some of the babies were killed in sacrificial ceremonies, like those recorded for eighteenth-century Natchez. When an important leader died, the surviving spouse would often slay one, or sometimes more, of their children out of respect and grief.

When a chief died, his servants were often killed and buried alongside his body, possibly because the Indians believed the chief would need their assistance in the next life. Later, this custom was also practiced by the Natchez Indians.

Continue south from Milepost 46. A sunken portion of the original Natchez Trace is on the right between Mileposts 42 and 41. You can get out of your car and walk along this deeply eroded path, which has seen the footprints of many different travelers. The surroundings are tangled and junglelike, with tall trees casting long shadows across the path. Tangles of gray moss drip from the branches, lending an air of mystery to the woods. The air is thick with the ever-present chirping of crickets, and though this high-pitched trill seems deafening at first, it quickly becomes pleasant white noise.

Imagine the thoughts of travelers walking in this same spot in the early 1800s. They, of course, did not have the luxury of returning to an air-conditioned vehicle. They were looking at a journey of some five hundred miles through stifling heat and humidity, steamy swamps, biting insects, poisonous snakes, and often-flooded rivers and streams. A misplaced step on a rock or an exposed root could lead to a twisted or broken ankle and a serious or even deadly situation.

Almost immediately after passing the Sunken Trace site, you will reach MS 18. Turn right onto this highway to reach the town of Port Gibson. It is 1.1 miles on MS 18 West to an intersection with U.S. 61. Turn left onto U.S. 61 South and drive into Port Gibson.

Located about a mile from the Trace, historic Port Gibson is named for its founder, Samuel Gibson. This lovely town, nestled in a crook of Bayou Pierre, was described by General Ulysses S. Grant as "too beautiful to burn." Port Gibson was a major objective in Grant's plan to seize Vicksburg in 1863. As you drive through this town of waxy-leafed magnolias, huge azaleas, and antebellum homes wrapped in porches, you will see that the town has not lost the charm that the Union general felt. Many of the homes and buildings here have been placed on the National Register of Historic Places.

If you are interested in staying overnight in one of Port Gibson's many bed-and-breakfast inns, stop by the chamber of commerce—located on U.S. 61 (Church Street) about 1.3 miles from MS 18—for information. The chamber is housed in the oldest home in Port Gibson, the Samuel Gibson House, built around 1805. You can also pick up brochures on self-guided auto tours of the historic district, along with a free foldout guide entitled *Claiborne County Historical Tours*, which maps out three excellent tours: "The Windsor-Battlefield Tour," "The Grand Gulf Tour," and "The Port Gibson Tour." This guide is an excellent resource for planning future visits.

On Church Street, one of the first things visitors notice is the church spire topped with a glistening golden hand pointing toward the heavens. This spire sits atop the pale-pink stucco First Presbyterian Church, one of the best-known structures in town. The hand is a tribute to the church's first pastor, the Reverend Butler, who was greatly respected and loved by his congregation. In memory of the pointing gesture that he often used in the pulpit, a huge wooden hand was carved and placed on the steeple. After years of exposure to the elements and woodpeckers, the hand was replaced with the golden model you see today.

If you peek inside the church, you will see chandeliers that came from the steamboat *Robert E. Lee.*

As you continue driving Church Street, you will quickly understand how the street got its name. Port Gibson is known as a city of churches; Church Street alone has eight.

When you have finished touring Port Gibson, retrace your route to the Natchez Trace Parkway and drive south. MS 552 intersects the parkway at Milepost 30, giving access to Canemount Plantation and Windsor Ruins to the west and Lorman to the east. A description of the area's accommodations and attractions is included in the following chapter.

Campground

NATCHEZ TRACE PARKWAY

Rocky Springs
Star Route, Box 14-C
Carlisle, MS 39049
(601) 535-7142

Located at Milepost 54.8, this campground is managed by the Natchez Trace Parkway. It offers twenty-two campsites and centrally located water and comfort stations.

Bed-and-Breakfast Inns

VICKSBURG

The Corners
601 Klein Street
Vicksburg, MS 39180
(800) 377-2770 or (615) 285-2777

Back in 1873, this beautiful mansion was built as a wedding present from father to daughter. Today, it is listed on the National Register of Historic Places. Only fifteen miles from the Trace, the inn is ideal for folks taking in the attractions of the parkway. There is a breathtaking view of the Mississippi River from a sixty-eight-foot-tall gallery. Each guest room is furnished with antiques and is also equipped with modern conveniences. Several rooms have fireplaces, which help create a romantic atmosphere on crisp autumn evenings. Full plantation breakfasts are included in the price of lodging.

Anchuca

1010 First East Street
Vicksburg, MS 39180
(601) 631-6800

This Greek Revival mansion, built around 1830, is conveniently located in the center of Vicksburg's historic district. It is beautifully furnished with period antiques and gas-burning chandeliers. A swimming pool, a cabana, and a Jacuzzi add a modern touch of luxury to your stay. *Country Inns of America* described Anchuca as "an exceptional inn—one of the finest inns to be found." Listed on the National Register of Historic Places, this inn has earned a four-diamond rating from the AAA Motor Club.

Anchuca is an Indian word for "happy home." This house once belonged to Joseph Davis, brother of the president of the Confederacy; it was from the balcony of Anchuca that Jefferson Davis delivered one of his moving speeches. Joseph Davis also owned the palatial Hurricane Plantation, which was burned by Union forces. Historians believe that the plantation was torched because the Yankees thought the magnificent home belonged to Jefferson Davis. In fact, Jefferson owned a much more modest home elsewhere.

The Balfour House

1002 Crawford Street
Vicksburg, MS 39180
(601) 638-7113

This bed-and-breakfast spot is open for tours. An exquisite spiral staircase sets this mansion apart from others.

In 1862, the owners, Dr. and Mrs. Balfour, were hosting an extravagant Christmas ball when a courier arrived to warn guests that Yankees were advancing on Vicksburg. Though many local women left their homes for the safety of hillside caves in the weeks to follow, Mrs. Balfour refused to leave her mansion. Her diary from the days of the siege has served as a important accounting of the final days before Vicksburg's capture.

Cedar Grove

2200 Oak Street
Vicksburg, MS 39180
(800) 448-2820 or (601) 636-2800

This home has more than a dozen rooms for overnight guests. Sitting high on a bluff, Cedar Grove overlooks the muddy waters of the Mississippi. If you choose to stay in this bed-and-breakfast, or if you just stop by for a tour, be sure to look for the cannonball lodged in the wall of the front parlor. It was left there as a reminder of the ordeal that Vicksburg residents endured back in 1863. The front door of this home also bore the brunt of cannon fire. It was ripped open by a cannonball and was never replaced, only repaired.

A relative of General William T. Sherman owned Cedar Grove during the Civil War. So it's not surprising to learn that this antebellum mansion and its lavish furnishings were untouched by Yankee hands. As we all know, blood is thicker than water.

Grey Oaks

4142 Rifle Range Road
Vicksburg, MS 39180
(601) 638-4424

One of the most noteworthy features of this bed-and-breakfast is the gardens, where a riot of colorful blossoms fights for space under a ceiling of latticed live-oak branches. In the late afternoon, splintered rays of yellow light steal their way past the huge tree trunks to light up pockets of green ravines.

The colorful gardens are beautiful, but the live oaks steal the show. Their twisted, ancient trunks seem bent into living sculptures. Mississippi writer Eudora Welty once wrote, "Perhaps the live oaks are the most wonderful trees in this land. Their great girth and their spread give far more feeling of history than any house or ruin left by man. It would be hard to think of things that happened here without the presence of these live oaks, so old, so expansive, so beautiful, that they might be sentient beings."

PORT GIBSON

Gibson's Landing
1002 Church Street
Port Gibson, MS 39150
(800) 377-2770 or (615) 285-2777

Built in 1830, this historic mansion is only two miles from the Trace. The architecture is an interesting combination of late Federal and early Greek Revival styles. The focal point of this beautiful inn is its spiral staircase, which climbs two and a half stories. All guest rooms are furnished with period antiques and tester beds. The suite has a private sun porch filled with wicker furniture. A full breakfast is offered in the morning.

Unique Dining

VICKSBURG

Velchoff's Corner
1101 Washington Street
Vicksburg, MS 39180
(601) 638-8661

The po-boy sandwiches and fried dill pickles at Velchoff's, housed in the old Uneeda Biscuit Warehouse, just shouldn't be missed.

Top o' the River
4150 Washington Street
Vicksburg, MS 39180
(601) 636-6262

As the name suggests, this restaurant overlooks the Mississippi River. But don't visit simply for the view. The heaping platters of fried catfish served here are "to die for."

Walnut Hills Restaurant

    1214 Adams Street
    Vicksburg, MS 39180
    (601) 638-4910

Eating here is like stopping by Grandma's for Sunday dinner after church. All of the home-cooked food is delicious, but the fried chicken is in a class by itself. It may be the best chicken in the South. And *that's* a tough superlative to earn.

Tuminello's

    500 Speed Street
    Vicksburg, MS 39180
    (601) 634-0507

This restaurant is housed in the former Tuminello's Grocery Store. Locals and visitors have been coming here since 1899 for fresh seafood and Italian food. In the fickle restaurant business, not many eateries can boast that kind of longevity.

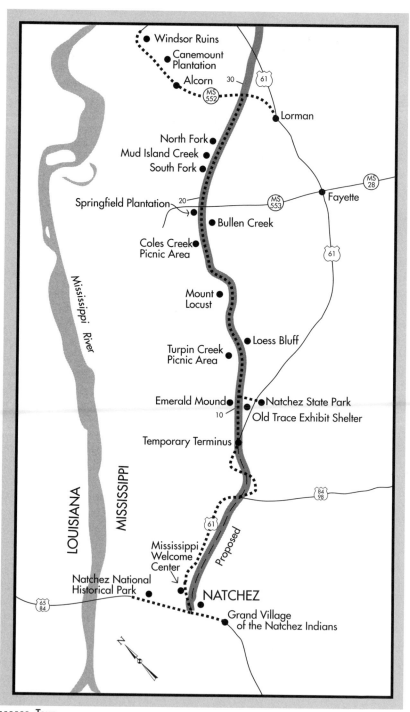

Windsor Ruins

Canemount
Plantation

Alcorn

30

US 61

MS 552

Lorman

North Fork

Mud Island Creek

South Fork

MS 28

Springfield Plantation

20

MS 553

Fayette

Bullen Creek

Coles Creek
Picnic Area

61

Mississippi River

Mount
Locust

Loess Bluff

Turpin Creek
Picnic Area

Emerald Mound

Natchez State Park

10

Old Trace Exhibit Shelter

Temporary Terminus

84
98

61

Proposed

Mississippi
Welcome
Center

NATCHEZ

MISSISSIPPI

LOUISIANA

Natchez National
Historical Park

65
84

Grand Village
of the Natchez Indians

N

WINDSOR RUINS

WINDSOR RUINS TO NATCHEZ

TOTAL MILEAGE
Approximately 70 miles
TOUR ENDPOINTS
This tour begins west of the parkway at Windsor Ruins, and ends in Natchez, Mississippi.

Milepost Guide

30.0 HIGHWAY INTERSECTION
MS 552 intersects the parkway here, giving travelers access from Windsor Ruins and Canemount Plantation to the west and Lorman to the east.

23.8 NORTH FORK
Picnic tables are located at this site.

22.1 MUD ISLAND CREEK
Picnic tables are located at this site.

21.2 SOUTH FORK
Picnic tables are also located at this site.

20.3   SPRINGFIELD PLANTATION

MS 553 intersects the parkway here and leads about one mile west to the plantation.

18.4   BULLEN CREEK

Here, a fifteen-minute nature trail winds through a mixed hardwood forest.

17.5   COLES CREEK PICNIC AREA

Picnic tables and rest rooms are located at this site.

15.5   MOUNT LOCUST

A restored historic house is located here. Interpretive programs are offered February through November. There are also exhibits, a ranger station, and rest rooms at this site.

12.4   LOESS BLUFF

12.1   TURPIN CREEK PICNIC AREA

Picnic tables are located here.

10.3   EMERALD MOUND/NATCHEZ STATE PARK

MS 553 intersects the parkway here and leads west less than a mile to Emerald Mound. The second-largest Indian burial mound of its type in the United States is located here. A trail leads to the top of the mound. MS 553 also leads two miles east from the parkway to Natchez State Park. A campground and picnic facilities are located here.

9.0   OLD TRACE EXHIBIT SHELTER

A section of the original Natchez Trace is located here.

8.1   TEMPORARY TERMINUS

The junction with U.S. 61 currently serves as the southern terminus of the parkway. U.S. 61 leads south approximately seven miles into Natchez.

The tour begins at Windsor Ruins, one of the most popular attractions near the Natchez Trace, located approximately ten miles west of the parkway via MS 552.

Windsor Plantation was named for the eerie music made by wind blowing through the capitals of the Corinthian columns located here. It was built by some six hundred slaves for an estimated $175,000. The figure was astonishingly high, but the owner, Smith Coffee Daniel II, was a wealthy planter with extensive landholdings in Mississippi and Louisiana. He could well afford the elaborate mansion.

At first glance, you might assume that these columns are the remains of a home burned to the ground by that dastardly Grant. However, Grant spared the structures in this area because of their beauty. Windsor Plantation was used as a headquarters by the Federals during the Civil War but was left intact when the troops moved on. Ironically, the house was destroyed by fire in 1890 by a careless smoker. Today, twenty-three weather-beaten columns are all that remain of the beautiful mansion that once graced this spot.

From Windsor Ruins, drive south on MS 552 toward Alcorn. Approximately 2.5 miles from the ruins, you will see Bethel Presbyterian Church on the left. This Greek Revival structure was built in 1845; the original congregation was organized in 1826. The interior of the church is very plain, with no embellishments or decorations. After the Civil War, the slave gallery was removed. The steeple that once sat atop the church was ripped off when a tornado swept through the area years ago.

Canemount Plantation, a six-thousand-acre working plantation, is on the left less than a mile past the church. Nestled in a beautiful rural setting, the house was built in 1855 and is considered the finest example of Italianate Revival architecture in Claiborne County. Historic cottages with fireplaces offer cozy hideaways for overnight guests searching for a respite from hectic workweeks. And though Canemount doesn't have the room to accommodate large groups overnight, it does offer lavish dinners and picnics for bike groups, church groups, and other big crowds. It is not uncommon for the owner to head into the woods in the morning, rifle in hand, to bag a Russian boar for the evening's pig roast. If you mention that you enjoy the outdoors, he might just suggest that you join him on a walk through the woods to flush a wild turkey, a white-tailed deer, or a feral hog. Guided hunts are also available in this private game preserve.

Continue following MS 552 from Canemount. It is 6.4 miles to the Natchez Trace Parkway. Drive under the parkway and continue straight for one mile to the intersection with U.S. 61. Turn right onto U.S. 61 and drive south. When you reach the intersection with eastbound MS 552, you will be in the town of Lorman. Here, you will find the Old Country Store, Lorman's claim to fame.

Built around 1890, this general store is a true Southern relic, so much so that it has been featured in newspapers and magazines such as the *St. Louis Post-Dispatch*, the *New Orleans Times-Picayune*, the *Birmingham Post-Herald*, *Southern Living*, *National Geographic*, *Better Homes and Gardens*, and many more.

The exterior looks like it hasn't seen a paintbrush in at least one hundred years. Old-fashioned red, white, and blue metal signs advertise Pepsi-Cola on the weathered, gray false front. When I stepped through the wide door, I immediately noticed a scent much like the one I smelled as a child when rummaging through the treasures in my grandmother's attic trunks. Pleasantly musty, it is the smell of something old that has been lovingly cared for. The scuffed longleaf-pine floors creak with every step, showing their age like an old man trying to straighten his arthritic back first thing in the morning.

An eclectic assortment of items is for sale: Shankstown bonnets—named for a former village on the Old Trace—shelled pecans, old newspapers, cast-iron skillets, overalls, ice cream, nails, books, twenty-five-cent grab bags, dolls, and even mellow hoop cheese sliced with an antique cheese cutter. Old-fashioned rolling ladders travel the length of the store, just in case you set your fancy on an item on the top shelf.

After visiting the Old Country Store, drive east on MS 552 for 2.5 miles to Rosswood Plantation. Begin slowing down when you see the white wooden fence and the Christmas-tree farm on the left.

Whether you are staying overnight or just taking an hour-long tour of this antebellum plantation, you will find the hosts at Rosswood gracious and accommodating. Back in 1849, this was a 1,250-acre cotton plantation worked by more than a hundred slaves. The white-columned mansion was built in 1857 by David Schroder, the same architect who built Windsor Plantation. It is a striking image of the Old South.

From Rosswood, return to U.S. 61 and retrace your route to the Natchez Trace Parkway. Head south on the parkway from Milepost 30.

As you make your final plunge toward Natchez, a treasure trove of historic sites and attractions fills the corridor of the parkway. Right away, you will come upon several picnic areas on Coles Creek. They are at North Fork, near Milepost 23; at Mud Island Creek, near Milepost 22; and at South Fork, near Milepost 21. All of these sites have picnic tables in shady settings which are perfect for an outdoor lunch or snack.

Just north of Milepost 20, MS 553 crosses the parkway. Exit here to reach Springfield Plantation, located about one mile west of the Trace. Follow the signs to the plantation.

Springfield Plantation was once owned by Thomas Green, a close friend of Rachel Donelson's family. It was here that Rachel fled to avoid a nasty confrontation with her estranged husband when she heard that he was coming to Nashville.

When Andrew Jackson got word of Rachel's separation in 1791, he immediately traveled to Springfield to ask for her hand. Controversy surrounded their marriage for the rest of their lives. Some say that Rachel's divorce from her first husband was never finalized. But till death did they part. Their love for and devotion to one another was unwavering and passionate.

The mansion at Springfield Plantation was one of the first in the United States to have a full-length, columned colonnade across the front. It was the first such house to be built in Mississippi. Unlike many of the South's mansions, whose interiors changed with restorations, Springfield remains almost entirely original.

Today, visitors are permitted to tour this working plantation. A walk down the lovely, old "quarter road" to a restored slave house is also interesting.

From Springfield Plantation, return to the Trace and continue south.

This stretch of parkway is exceptionally beautiful. At times, a twist of the pavement leads under a canopy of live oaks; it looks like the limbs have strained to reach across the road and tightly grab hold of one another. These evergreens are especially beautiful in winter against the bare branches of surrounding deciduous trees. From a distance, their romantic silhouettes are unmistakable. With their leaves like verdant petticoats and their delicately curving branches, they are decidedly the most feminine of all trees.

The last nature trail on the parkway is coming up at Bullen Creek, between Mileposts 19 and 18. This is your final chance to take a short walk through these beautiful Southern woods. Pinched between a mixed forest of gangly pines and leafy hardwoods, the trail gives visitors a scenic, easy fifteen-minute hike. Again, you are sure to notice the live oaks. Uncommonly strong and durable, many of these trees are hundreds of years old. High rainfall and humidity nourish the mighty oaks, their trunks expanding to massive girths while their huge limbs spread wide. Few images more vividly represent the Deep South than a great oak draped in Spanish moss.

After passing Coles Creek Picnic Area, located between Mileposts 18 and 17, you will approach one of the most popular attractions on the entire Natchez Trace Parkway: Mount Locust.

Of the many primitive stands that sprang up along the Old Trace during its heyday as a national road, Mount Locust is the only one still standing. This structure, one of the oldest in Mississippi, was built back in 1780. In order to fulfill a land grant issued by the British government of West Florida, Thomas Harmon constructed this single-room cabin.

Not long after the cabin was built, it changed hands several times before William Ferguson became the owner. With a growing family to house, he soon made additions to the one-room building. He also found himself providing lodging for homebound Kaintucks here at Mount Locust. It was not his intention to establish an inn, but the location of his house—a full day's walk from Natchez—kept the boatmen knocking on his front door. When Ferguson envisioned the distance they still had to travel over the next weeks, he didn't have the heart to turn them away.

As business grew, Ferguson built a four-room, two-story annex behind the main house; this annex came to be known as "Sleepy Hollow."

With increased traffic and prosperity along the Natchez Trace, Ferguson and four neighbors organized a township. They mapped out a village and sold lots. It wasn't long before businesses sprang up in this little hamlet. Soon, local residents had a doctor, a cabinetmaker, storekeepers, a brickmaker, a tanner, and others. The town even had an early cotton gin.

The grounds of Mount Locust are open year-round, but the house is open for tours only from February through November. During those months, a National Park Service ranger is on-site to provide information. This old frontier homestead is furnished with the types of items used by Trace travelers. Rather than simply assembling a mix of antiques, the park service has done an excellent job of replicating the appearance and atmosphere of the interior of the old homestead and inn.

Loess Bluff, a nature area located south of Milepost 13, tells an interesting story of windblown topsoil from the Ice Age. When glaciers covered the northern half of America, endless dust storms swirled into this area from the western plains. Some of the deposits of soil, called loess, were as thick as thirty to ninety feet. Because the soil was so loose, it was especially prone to erosion. In spots where the Old Trace passed the loess bluffs, some sections of trail sank to depths of nearly twenty feet.

Not far from Loess Bluff is Turpin Creek Picnic Area. Located near Milepost 12, this is the last spot on the Natchez Trace Parkway where picnic tables and charcoal grills can be found.

Less than two miles past Turpin Creek Picnic Area, you will reach an intersection with MS 553. Exit the parkway and turn right, or west, to access Emerald Mound. You will reach a sharp curve in the road; drive straight on Emerald Mound Road. The mound is located on the right about one mile from the Trace.

Covering nearly eight acres, Emerald Mound is the second-largest Indian mound in the entire United States surpassed only by Monk's Mound in Illinois. It is believed that this mound and others once located here were built sometime around 1300 A.D. by the Mississippian Indians—predecessors of the now-extinct Natchez nation. The Bear Creek and Owl Creek mounds discussed earlier are generally of the same culture and time period. Unlike mounds built for burials, these flat-topped mounds served as the focal point of the Mississippian Indians' villages. It was on top of the mounds that ceremonial dances took place, religious rituals were enacted, games were played, and more.

It wasn't until the 1930s that the mound was called Emerald Mound. Before that, the complex of mounds was known as

Selsertown Mounds, named for a now-extinct village.

If you like, you can walk up the path to the top of the mound. From that vantage, your imagination can slip easily to the days so long ago when Indian feet dusted this very spot.

To reach Natchez State Park from Emerald Mound, return to where MS 553 intersects the Natchez Trace Parkway. Drive straight across the Trace and continue on MS 553 to U.S. 61. Proceed straight across U.S. 61 and follow the signs to the park, which is about one mile away.

Twenty-one tent campsites are offered at Natchez State Park. There are also cabins, a picnic area, and a nature trail. Fishermen and watersports enthusiasts will enjoy the large lake here. Hamburg Road, an old plantation road, runs through the park.

From Natchez State Park, return to the Trace and continue south. The last stop on the parkway is at Milepost 9, where you will find an exhibit on the Old Trace. Photographs and maps at this site trace the history and development of the old trail. Interpretive exhibits outline the highlights found along this famous frontier road.

The temporary terminus of the Natchez Trace Parkway is just ahead, near Milepost 8. Exit onto U.S. 61 to drive into the city of Natchez.

Be sure to save time for touring a few of the city's mansions. Natchez is famous for its wealth of antebellum homes, remnants of a gracious age in Southern history. These homes call to mind the days of handsome horse-drawn carriages, hoop skirts and taffeta, snipped magnolia blossoms floating in water-filled crystal bowls, and the call of a steamboat whistle. The years blur as you step through their welcoming front doors into a place where time seems to have stopped and grand traditions prevail. Come along as we step back in time in Natchez, the oldest and final city on the Natchez Trace.

Hundreds of years before the first antebellum house was built, this area was home to tribes of mound-building, sun-worshiping Indians who lived in small villages. They were the Natchez Indians, for whom the city was named. Then, in 1716, French explorers arrived and established a garrison called Fort Rosalie. After the French and Indian War, the area fell under British rule. But during the American Revolution, England was preoccupied with holding onto the original thirteen colonies and lost the area to Spain. The United States finally claimed the region from Spain under treaty in 1798.

From the early 1800s to the Civil War, Natchez was a bustling river port. Steamboats pushed and shoved their way to the crowded docks. Traders poured money into the town as they drank whiskey, gambled, visited brothels, and lived it up in the infamous Natchez Under-the-Hill. Money flowed, attracting more than half of the millionaires in all of America to come to Natchez to live. Plantation owners prospered with lucrative cotton crops. As a testament to their wealth, elaborate mansions sprang up all over the city. Marble was imported from Italy, fine bone china arrived from France, and rich fabrics and intricate lace were shipped from Europe to fashion ball dresses for the ladies of high society. King Cotton reigned, and Mississippi was regarded as one of the wealthiest states in the country.

Then, on an early-spring morning in 1861, hundreds of miles away in Charleston, South Carolina, Southern cannons opened fire on Fort Sumter. The Civil War had begun. Life in Natchez was about to change in a big way.

With no railroads, Natchez had little military significance and never suffered the ravages of battle. For the most part, it simply waited out the storm while holding its breath and hoping for the best. In the end, the city survived the war essentially unscathed, but the aftermath was great. The opulent homes and huge mansions were spared, but the economy was in ruins.

The war brought the busy river trade on the Mississippi to a grinding halt. After the slaves were emancipated and the Confederacy fell, there weren't enough hands to work the land. This region, once graced with opulence, was now crippled by poverty. The golden era was over.

The plantation owners' loss may have been our gain, however. Oddly enough, the postwar financial ruin has been credited with preserving Natchez's architectural treasures. While the rest of the world was responding to fads and exploring new building styles, the residents of Natchez had to just make do. They had no money for renovations to keep up with changing styles.

Ironically, Natchez began pulling out of its economic slump in 1932, during the Great Depression. It began as a fluke, really. The women of the city were preparing for a state convention of garden clubs, to be held in Natchez. Just days before guests were to arrive to tour the magnificent gardens, a freak late frost blanketed the area.

Every last blossom and bud was turned into a sparkling, frozen disaster. The gardens were completely wiped out.

The women were panic-stricken. How could they possibly host garden tours now? Then someone suggested opening the mansions themselves to the visitors. But with money so tight, many of the homes had fallen into disrepair.

So, just as Scarlett ripped down the green velvet parlor draperies of war-stricken Tara to make a new gown for her meeting with Rhett, the matrons of Natchez went to work polishing silver, cleaning windows, and scrubbing wooden floors. Tattered draperies were mended and worn spots in upholstered furniture were covered with colorful needlepoint pillows. By the time the first door was swung wide, the grand homes gleamed. The response was overwhelming. The tradition of the Spring Pilgrimage was born.

It wasn't long before the entire country heard of Natchez's wealth of unaltered plantations. Tourists flocked to see the splendid antebellum mansions and glimpse the South's romantic past. The Pilgrimage turned into an annual event and was so successful that neighboring cities and states followed suit. Tourism became big business, turning the economy around.

There are so many antebellum mansions in Natchez that a bevy of guidebooks has been devoted to the city's historic sites alone. Some of the most popular historic homes are highlighted in this chapter. All five mansions covered here are open to tourists year-round. Most of these antebellum homes are found within an area bordered by Broadway, Washington, Union, and High streets, and quite a few of them have become bed-and-breakfast inns.

To begin your sightseeing in Natchez, follow U.S. 61 South for 7.2 miles after exiting the parkway; turn left at the traffic signal to continue on U.S. 61 South/U.S. 84 West. The Mississippi Welcome Center is located on the right after 0.1 mile. Continue 1.9 miles, then turn right onto Melrose Avenue/Montebello Parkway at the sign for Natchez National Historical Park. Drive 0.9 mile to the turnoff to the park, which is on the right.

The Natchez National Historical Park is managed by the National Park Service, as is the Natchez Trace Parkway. The historical park covers most of the town of Natchez. Everything except Melrose Mansion, the hilltop site of Fort Rosalie, and the William Johnson

House, is privately owned, but the National Park Service provides technical assistance for the preservation of the historical properties. For more information about the Natchez National Historical Park, contact the superintendent at (601) 442-7047.

Melrose Mansion, one of the first homes to be included in the original Pilgrimage, is located in Natchez National Historical Park. Built around 1845, this mansion is now a National Historic Land-mark. Melrose is a beautiful blend of Greek Revival and Georgian architecture. Named for Scotland's Melrose Abbey, the mansion was the suburban estate of a lawyer and planter from Pennsylvania named John T. McMurran. Although he owned cotton plantations in Louisiana and other parts of Mississippi, McMurran never used the land at Melrose to grow cotton.

The estate now encompasses nearly eighty acres. Inside the mansion, you will see Italian marble fireplaces, hand-carved Victorian furnishings, and several rare, painted English floorcloths. When touring the home, be sure to notice the chairs in the Green Parlor. The design of Gorham's "Melrose" silver pattern is almost identical to the design of the chair backs.

ROSALIE MANSION

Dennis Coello

STANTON HALL

TRAVELING THE NATCHEZ TRACE

Also located on the grounds of the park are several outbuildings that served as a kitchen and living quarters for house slaves in years gone by. Visitors have an opportunity to examine a smokehouse, two cisterns, a formal garden, a slavery exhibit featuring a re-created slave residence, a typical antebellum stable, and a carriage house.

After leaving Natchez National Historical Park, return to U.S. 61/ U.S. 84 and turn left. Drive 1.2 miles, then turn right onto Liberty Road to reach downtown Natchez. You will drive under a bridge to a fork; bear left. You will then come to a stop sign; proceed straight through. Sitting high on a hill on the left is beautiful Monmouth Plantation. Continue straight on John Quitman Parkway, which becomes Main Street after about 0.5 mile.

Follow Main Street through the downtown area until you reach Canal Street. Turn left and drive one block to the Natchez Pilgrimage Tours Headquarters, located on the corner of Canal and State streets. Here, you can pick up a free walking-tour map and lists of historic homes open for tours. If you are visiting the city during the annual Spring and Fall pilgrimages, you are in luck. During those events, more than thirty homes and mansions throw open their doors to visitors.

From the Natchez Pilgrimage Tours Headquarters, drive south on Canal Street for a block or two to Orleans Street and turn right to see Rosalie Mansion, located on the right at 100 Orleans.

This imposing brick mansion sits on the Natchez Bluff overlooking the Mississippi River. It was named for the French fort built by the governor of Louisiana in 1716; that fort once loomed on the hilltop behind the mansion. It was there that the Natchez Indians massacred the French garrison back in 1729.

When Rosalie was built in 1823, the image of a perfect Southern mansion was established. The home's white columns, red bricks, and hip roof give it a classic antebellum look. The beautiful furnishings, bought in 1858, include a famous Belter parlor set.

Rosalie did its part during the Civil War, serving as the local headquarters for Union forces. Today, it is a registered National Historic Landmark.

From Rosalie, turn left onto Canal Street and drive north about six blocks to High Street. Turn right onto High; the Interstate Coffee Company is on the corner. Drive several blocks to Stanton Hall, located on the left at 401 High.

One of the most-photographed houses in the United States, Stanton Hall was built in 1857, covering an entire city block. Today, it remains one of the largest antebellum mansions in America and is a National Historic Landmark.

Flanking the front of this palatial house are four fluted columns. Lacy wrought-iron railings enclose two porticoes. Inside, the hallway stretches an impressive seventy feet, and the ceilings are more than sixteen feet high. The famous Carriage House Restaurant is located across a courtyard filled with hundreds of gorgeous azaleas and stately old trees.

After touring Stanton Hall, turn right off High Street onto Commerce Street. Drive several blocks to Orleans Street and turn left. After one block, turn right onto Union Street. Ravennaside Mansion is located at the end of the road at 601 South Union.

One of Natchez's most significant examples of Colonial Revival architecture, Ravennaside was built for entertaining by a local socialite couple around 1870. Beautiful stained glass, hand-tinted wallpaper, and decorative parquet floors highlight Ravennaside. Of special interest is the Gold Room, where dignitaries, politicians, and other important guests were wined and dined in years past. Ravennaside is listed on the National Register of Historic Places.

From Ravennaside, return to Orleans Street and turn right. This street becomes Homochitto Street in less than 0.2 mile; continue straight. At the intersection with U.S. 84/U.S. 98, drive straight across and continue on Lower Woodville Road. The turnoff for Longwood Mansion, located at 140 Lower Woodville, is on the right.

A winding dirt road leads visitors on a gorgeous, short drive from Lower Woodville Road to the mansion. This is perhaps the most unusual home in town. If you could only see one antebellum structure while in Natchez, Longwood would be my recommendation.

The very wealthy Dr. Haller Nutt began building this mansion before the Civil War. Carpenters who hailed from the North were hard at work on the house when word arrived that war had broken out. Tossing their hammers and nails aside, the Yankees broke into a sprint and hightailed it home to Mama. (Actually, they probably went to enlist, but we Southerners prefer the first version of the story.) Poor Dr. Nutt was left with an unfinished mansion and died before he could complete it. Today, the house is still unfinished. The home of the Pilgrimage Garden Club, Longwood is the largest octagonal house in America. It is also a National Historic Landmark.

Though these magnificent mansions offer a glimpse of the past, Natchez's roots go much deeper. To reach the Grand Village of the Natchez Indians from Longwood Mansion, return to the intersection with U.S. 84. Turn right onto U.S. 84 and drive to the junction with U.S. 61; the hospital will be on your right. Bear right on U.S. 61 and follow the signs for the Grand Village of the Natchez Indians; turn left onto Highland Boulevard and drive 0.6 mile to the village, located on the right.

Long before the first Southern belle sashayed across the white-columned veranda of an antebellum home, this area was inhabited by a much different native: the mysterious Natchez Indian. Sometime in the late 1600s, the Grand Village of the Natchez Indians was established on the banks of St. Catherine Creek just outside what is now the city of Natchez. This was during the height of the Indians' occupation of this area.

According to the faded journals of visiting Frenchmen, priests,

GRAND VILLAGE OF THE NATCHEZ INDIANS

and journalists, the Grand Village was an elaborate ceremonial center. The culture and customs of the Natchez Indians were complex and sophisticated. In fact, theirs was the most advanced civilization north of the Mayan and Aztec tribes of Central America and Mexico. Ceremonies and religious rituals were of supreme importance to the Natchez Indians, and it was at the Grand Village that these ceremonies were centered.

An advanced social structure was in evidence in the Natchez nation. Four classes were acknowledged: suns, nobles, honored people, and "stinkards," or commoners. Strict rules regarding marriage between the classes were observed. The ruler of all the people was the Great Sun, or chief. When he died, his wives were strangled and laid to rest with him for his pleasure in the afterlife. (After being strangled to death, I doubt they were in the mood to give him much "pleasure" for at least a few millennia!)

The bones of past chiefs were enshrined inside the sacred temple of the Grand Village. A holy fire burned perpetually in the temple's center as a symbol of the Great Sun. Chosen tribesmen attended the fire at all times. If it ever went out, the guilty tribesman was to be killed.

Unlike other tribes, the Natchez people did not have a need for tight concentration of their villages; a French explorer reported some thirty scattered villages in 1703. The walls of the Natchez Indians' huts were of wattle-and-daub construction, and the roofs were made of straw thatch. Because of the warm climate, extremely sturdy housing materials were not needed. However, the intense heat of summer made the construction of the roof especially important; shelter from the sun was critical for comfort and survival.

The French settled in the land of the Natchez nation in the early 1700s. Initially, relations between the two groups were good, but they deteriorated from 1716 to 1729. In 1729, the Indians launched a brutal attack on the garrison at Fort Rosalie. The French later retaliated and completely destroyed the Grand Village. Most of the Indians were killed during the massacre, though a few escaped into the forest. It is believed that they fled to the land of the Chickasaws— their allies—and eventually became part of that people. By 1730, the entire nation of Natchez Indians had vanished.

Today, visitors to the Grand Village of the Natchez Indians can see the famed ceremonial mound, a reconstructed hut, and interpretive

A CHURCH IN NATCHEZ

exhibits that chronicle the daily lives of the Natchez people. A museum displays artifacts excavated from the mounds and the surrounding area. A gift shop features Indian-related items, souvenirs, and books. Nature trails weave through the property. A picnic area is also provided.

Before winding up your tour of this final city on the Natchez Trace Parkway, make your way to the riverfront to see the marker erected by the Daughters of the American Revolution back in 1909. This simple marker stands at the true southern terminus of the Natchez Trace. Eventually, the National Park Service will extend the parkway all the way into Natchez to a point near this spot.

To reach the marker from the Grand Village of the Natchez Indians,

Windsor Ruins to Natchez

return to U.S. 61 and drive north for several miles to the Liberty Road turnoff. Head right on Liberty Road to return to the historic downtown area. You will drive under a bridge to a fork; bear left. You will then come to a stop sign; proceed straight through. Continue straight on John Quitman Parkway, which becomes Main Street after about 0.5 mile. Drive to the end of Main Street, cross Canal Street, and park on Broadway Street. The marker is on a large rock surrounded by a black iron fence.

As you gaze across the muddy waters of the Mississippi and then turn to the north and think back on all the miles you have covered since leaving Nashville, imagine the thoughts of a boatman as he stood on this same riverbank and planned his journey home on the Trace. To think of actually walking this old frontier road, especially as a matter of course, is truly incredible.

Campground

NATCHEZ

Natchez State Park
230-B Wickliff Road
Natchez, MS 39120
(601) 442-2658

This state-managed campground offers twenty-four campsites, two cabins, hookups, showers, rest rooms, picnic areas, and nature trails. It is located two miles east of the parkway off U.S. 61.

Bed-and-Breakfast Inns

LORMAN

Canemount Plantation
MS 552 West, Lorman
MS 39096
(800) 423-0684 or (601) 445-3784

Located halfway between Vicksburg and Natchez, this plantation offers historic cottages with fireplaces or wood-burning stoves. Guided nature tours through surrounding fields and woods are offered. If you are interested in photography, your hosts will show you good areas to shoot wildlife. If you are more interested in shooting wildlife with a rifle or a shotgun on this private game preserve, guided hunts are available in season. A heated swimming pool is also located on the plantation.

Rosswood Plantation

MS 552 East
Lorman, MS 39096
(800) 377-2770 or (615) 285-2777

If you're afraid of ghosts, you'd better find another place to stay, because Rosswood Plantation boasts a resident ghoul! Dating from about 1857, this home was built in the Greek Revival style. High ceilings, winding stairways, spacious guest rooms, and columned galleries add to its appeal. The original slave quarters still stand on this plantation. While you are sure to appreciate the age of this historic house, you will also welcome modern conveniences such as a heated pool, a Jacuzzi, televisions, and telephones. For a trip down history's storied lane, you can sit down and read the diary that belonged to an early owner of the house. Children are welcome here.

NATCHEZ

Sweet Olive Tree Manor

700 Orleans Street
Natchez, MS 39120
(800) 377-2770 or (615) 285-2777

This Victorian manor is furnished with beautiful antiques. Built in 1880, it is right at home in its historic Garden District location, within walking distance of other antebellum homes and historic sites. Late in the afternoon, tea, wine, and cheese are served to guests in the parlor. Sumptuous gourmet breakfasts are served in the formal dining room.

Governor Holmes' House

207 South Wall Street
Natchez, MS 39120
(800) 377-2770 or (615) 285-2777

As the home of the last governor of the Mississippi territory and
the first governor of the state of Mississippi, Governor Holmes' House
is one of the most historic sites in Natchez. Built in 1794, it is also
one of the oldest. Not surprisingly, the house is listed on the National Register of Historic Places.

The home is beautifully decorated with period antiques, paintings, Oriental carpets, and fine porcelain pieces. A full plantation
breakfast of fresh eggs, spicy sausage, creamy grits, and biscuits is
served to guests in the morning.

Hope Farm

147 Homochitto Street
Natchez, MS 39120
(800) 377-2770 or (615) 285-2777

Featured in *Southern Living*, this home was once owned by the
first Spanish governor of the Mississippi territory. It was built sometime between 1774 and 1789. Antique furniture dating back to the
eighteenth century is found throughout the home. Distinctive four-
poster beds with draped testers grace the guest rooms. Each room
also has a private bath. And of course, a full Southern breakfast is
served in the formal dining room. The house is surrounded by twenty
acres of beautiful gardens, and Natchez City Park is only a short
distance away.

NATCHEZ

Monmouth Plantation

John A. Quitman Parkway
P.O. Box 1736
Natchez, MS 39121
(800) 828-4531 or (601) 442-5852

For a true taste of the Old South, make a reservation for an elegant plantation dinner served in the historic dining room of this antebellum mansion.

Carriage House Restaurant

401 High Street
Natchez, MS 39120
(601) 445-5151

This restaurant, located on the grounds of historic Stanton Hall, is famous for its mint juleps and Southern fried chicken. It is open only for lunch most of the year. During the Spring and Fall pilgrimages, it also opens for dinner.

Clara Nell's Downtown Delicatessen

609A Franklin Street
Natchez, MS 39120
(601) 445-7799

This deli is a great lunch spot if you are looking for a thick sandwich or a bowl of homemade soup. Clara Nell's also has daily lunch specials and delicious casseroles.

Appendix

Chambers of Commerce and Other Tourist Agencies

Canton Convention and
Visitors Bureau
P.O. Box 53
Canton, MS 39046
800-844-3369 or 601-859-1307

Corinth-Alcorn Chamber
of Commerce
810 Tate Street
Corinth, MS 38834
601-287-5269

Jackson Convention and
Visitors Bureau
P.O. Box 1450
Jackson, MS 39215
800-354-7695 or 601-960-1891

Kosciusko Chamber
of Commerce
301 East Jefferson Street
P.O. Box 696
Kosciusko, MS 39090
601-289-2981

Lawrenceburg Chamber of
Commerce
U.S. 43 North
P.O. Box 86
Lawrenceburg, TN 38464
615-762-4911

Lewis County Chamber of
Commerce
P.O. Box 182
Hohenwald, TN 38462
615-796-4084

Majestic Middle Tennessee
Fall Tour
P.O. Box 942
Columbia, TN 38402
800-381-1865 or
615-381-7176

Maury County Convention
and Visitors Bureau
308 West Seventh Street
P.O. Box 1076
Columbia, TN 38402
800-381-1865 or
615-381-7176

Nashville Convention and
Visitors Bureau
161 Fourth Avenue North
Nashville, TN 37219
615-259-3900

Natchez Convention and
Visitor's Bureau
P.O. Box 1485
422 Main Street
Natchez, MS 39121-1485
800-647-6724

Natchez Trace Bed-and-
Breakfast Reservation Service
P.O. Box 193
Hampshire, TN 38461
800-377-2770 or 615-285-2777

Port Gibson/Claiborne
County Chamber of
Commerce
P.O. Box 491
Port Gibson, MS 39150
601-437-4351

Shoals Chamber of Commerce
104 South Pine Street
Florence, AL 35630
205-764-4661

Starkville Visitors and
Convention Council
P.O. Box 2720
322 University Drive
Starkville, MS 39759
601-323-3322

Tennessee Fall Color Hotline
800-636-8900

Tupelo Convention and Visitors
Bureau
P.O. Drawer 47
Tupelo, MS 38802-0047
800-533-0611 or 601-841-6521

Vicksburg Convention and
Visitors Bureau
P.O. Box 110
Vicksburg, MS 39181
800-221-3536 or 601-636-9421

Williamson County Chamber of
Commerce and Tourism Center
P.O. Box 156
109 Second Avenue South
Franklin, TN 37604
615-794-1225

Attractions, Historic Sites, and Museums

Athenaeum
808 Athenaeum Street
P.O. Box 942
Columbia, TN 38402
615-381-4822

Belle Meade Plantation
5025 Harding Road
Nashville, TN 37205
615-356-0501

Carnton Plantation and
Confederate Cemetery
  1345 Carnton Lane
  Franklin, TN 37064
  615-794-0903

Carter House
  1140 Columbia Avenue
  Franklin, TN 37064
  615-791-1861

Curlee House
  301 Childs Street
  Corinth, MS 38834
  601-287-2231

David Crockett State Museum
  South Locust Avenue
  Lawrenceburg, TN 38464
  615-762-9408

Elvis Presley Birthplace and
Museum
  306 Elvis Presley Drive
  Tupelo, MS 38802
  601-841-1245

Eudora Welty Library
  300 North State Street
  Jackson, MS 39202
  601-968-5811

Gentry's General Store
  2997 Oktoc Road
  Starkville, MS 39759
  601-323-1278

Governor's Mansion
  300 East Capitol Street
  Jackson, MS 39202
  601-359-3175

Grand Village of the Natchez
Indians
  400 Jefferson Davis Boulevard
  Natchez, MS 39121
  601-446-6502

Hammond-Routte House
  109 South Natchez Drive
  Kosciusko, MS 39090
  800-323-1039 or 601-289-4131

The Hermitage
  4580 Rachel's Lane
  Hermitage, TN 37076
  615-889-2941

Hohenwald Train Depot
  112 East Main Street
  Hohenwald, TN 38462
  615-796-4084

Indian Mound Museum
  South Court Street
  Florence, AL 35630
  205-760-6427

Ivy Green
  300 West North Commons
  Tuscumbia, AL 35674
  205-383-4066

Jackson City Hall
  219 South President Street
  Jackson, MS 39202
  601-960-1084

Jackson Zoological Park
  2918 West Capitol Street
  Jackson, MS 39205
  601-352-2580

James K. Polk House
301 West Seventh Street
P.O. Box 741
Columbia, TN 38402
615-388-2354

Jim Buck Ross Mississippi
Agriculture and Forestry
Museum/National
Agricultural Aviation
Museum
1150 Lakeland Drive
Jackson, MS 39216
800-844-TOUR or
601-354-6113

Joseph Biedenharn
Museum
1107 Washington Street
Vicksburg, MS 39180
601-638-6514

Lakemont
1103 Main Street
Vicksburg, MS 39180
601-636-9421

Lewis County Museum
112 East Main Street
Hohenwald, TN 38462
615-796-4084

Longwood Mansion
140 Lower Woodville Road
Natchez, MS 39121
601-442-5193

Manship House
420 East Fortification Street
Jackson, MS 39202
601-961-4724

Martha Vick House
1300 Grove Street
Vicksburg, MS 39180
601-638-7036

Mississippi Crafts Center
Natchez Trace Parkway
Ridgeland, MS 39157
601-856-7546

Mississippi Museum of Art
201 East Pascagoula Street
Jackson, MS 39202
601-960-1515

Mississippi Museum of
Natural Science
111 North Jefferson Street
Jackson, MS 39202
601-354-7303

Mississippi State University's
Enology Lab and Dairy Science
Center
P.O. Box 9630
Mississippi State, MS 39762
601-325-2323

Mississippi War Memorial
Building
120 South State Street
Jackson, MS 39202
601-354-7207

Mount Locust
c/o Natchez Trace
    Parkway Headquarters
Rural Route 1, NT-143
Tupelo, MS 38801
601-842-1572

Mule Day Celebration
308 West Seventh Street
P.O. Box 66
Columbia, TN 38402
615-381-9557

Mynelle Gardens
4736 Clinton Boulevard
Jackson, MS 39209
601-960-1894 or 601-960-1814

Natchez National Historical Park
P.O. Box 1208
Natchez, MS 39121
601-446-5790

Northeast Mississippi Museum
P.O. Box 993
Corinth, MS 38834
601-287-3120

The Oaks House Museum
823 North Jefferson Street
Jackson, MS 39202
601-353-9339

Old Capitol Museum
100 South State Street
Jackson, MS 39202
601-359-6920

Old Country Store
P.O. Box 217
Lorman, MS 39096
601-437-3661

Old Court House Museum
1008 Cherry Street
Vicksburg, MS 39180
601-636-0741

Old Jail Museum
Noxubee County Library
103 East King Street
Macon, MS 39341
601-726-5461

Oprah Winfrey's Birthplace
Oprah Winfrey Road
P.O. Box 696
Kosciusko, MS 39090

Pickwick Landing Dam
TN 128
Pickwick Dam, TN 38365
901-925-4346

Pope's Tavern
203 Hermitage Drive
Florence, AL 35630
205-760-6439

Rattle and Snap Plantation
c/o Maury County Convention
and Visitors Bureau
P.O. Box 1076
Mount Pleasant, TN 38402
800-381-1865 or 615-381-7176

Ravennaside
601 South Union Street
Natchez, MS 39121
601-442-8015

Rosalie Mansion
100 Orleans Street
Natchez, MS 39121
601-445-4555

Russell C. Davis Planetarium
201 East Pascagoula Street
Jackson, MS 39202
601-960-1550

Smith-Robertson Museum
and Cultural Center
528 Bloom Street
Jackson, MS 39202
601-960-1457

Springfield Plantation
Route 1, Box 201
Fayette, MS 39069
601-786-3802

Stanton Hall
401 High Street
Natchez, MS 39121
800-647-6742 or
601-446-6631

Sunshine Farms
Route 1, Box 92
Macon, MS 39341
601-726-2264

Tupelo Museum
Highway 6 West at James L.
Ballard Park
Tupelo, MS 38802
601-841-6438

W. C. Handy Museum
620 West College Street
Florence, AL 35630
205-760-6434

Windsor Ruins
c/o Port Gibson/Claiborne
County Chamber of Commerce
P. O. Box 491
Port Gibson, MS 39150
601-437-4351

Yesterday's Children Doll
Museum and Shop
1104 Washington Street
Vicksburg, MS 39180
601-638-0650

Natural Areas and State Parks

Buffalo River Canoeing
18 West Linden Street
Hohenwald, TN 38462
615-796-3622

Casey Jones Museum
State Park
10901 Vaughan Road
Vaughan, MS 39179
601-673-9864

David Crockett State Park
Lawrenceburg, TN 38464
615-762-9408 (office) or
615-762-9541 (restaurant)

Mississippi Petrified Forest
P.O. Box 37
Flora, MS 39071-0037
601-879-8189

Noxubee National Wildlife
Refuge
    Route 1, Box 142
    Brooksville, MS 39739
    601-323-5548

Pickwick Landing State Park
    TN 57 South and TN 128
    Pickwick Dam, TN 38365
    901-689-3129

Tishomingo State Park
    P.O. Box 880
    Tishomingo, MS 38873
    601-438-6914

National Park Service Offices

Jeff Busby
    Route 3, Box 80-A
    Ackerman, MS 39735
    601-387-4365

Meriwether Lewis Site
    Route 3, Box 368
    Hohenwald, TN 38462
    615-796-2675

Natchez Trace Parkway
Headquarters
    Rural Route 1, NT-143
    Tupelo, MS 38801
    601-680-4025 or
    800-305-7417

Rocky Springs Site
    Star Route, Box 14-C
    Carlisle, MS 39049
    601-535-7142

National Military Parks

Brices Cross Roads National
Battlefield Site
    c/o National Park Service
    R.R. 1, NT-143
    Tupelo, MS 38801

Shiloh National Military Park
    TN 22 South
    Shiloh, TN 38376
    901-689-5696

Tupelo National Battlefield Site
    c/o National Park Service
    R.R. 1, NT-143
    Tupelo, MS 38801

Vicksburg National
Military Park
    3201 Clay Street
    Vicksburg, MS 39180
    601-636-0583

Index

Sturgis, Samuel D., 93
Sullivan, Anne, 60, 61
Sumter, Fort, 203
Sunken Trace, 41, 50, 174, 187
Sunshine Farms, 120
Swan Valley Overlook, 22, 31
Sweet Olive Tree Mansion, 213
Sweetwater Branch, 40, 50
Sweetwater Inn, 36

Taft, William Howard, 11
Tennessee Game and Fish Com-
  mission, 46
Tennessee General Assembly, 48
Tennessee River, 14, 56, 57, 58,
  62, 64, 66, 71, 72, 83, 89
Tennessee Valley, 56
Tennessee Valley Authority, 64, 71
Tennessee Valley Divide, 4, 14
Tennessee/Alabama state line, 39,
  41, 50
Tennessee-Tombigbee Waterway
  ("Tenn-Tom"), 87, 89, 90
Tennessee's Antebellum Trail, 23
Texas, 48, 49, 78, 122, 175
Third Louisiana Infantry, 178
Thompson, Polly, 61
Tishomingo Creek Bridge, 93
Tishomingo State Park, 69, 70,
  82, 87, 89, 97
Tobacco Farm, 22, 29, 30, 31
Tockshish, 100, 106
Tombigbee National Forest, 107,
  111
Tombigbee Prairie, 105
Tombigbee River, 89, 96, 107
Tombigbee State Park, 110
Top o' the River, 192
Trail of Tears, 31, 106
Trail of the Big Trees, 118
Treaty of Dancing Rabbit Creek,
  64, 124, 137
Treaty of Doak's Stand, 147, 169,
  185
Treaty of Paris, 151
Treaty of Pontitock Creek, 106
Trolio Hotel, 145, 154
Trolio, Peter, 154

Trolio, Vic, 154
Trolio's Bourbon, 154
Tuminello's Grocery Store, 193
Tuminello's Restaurant, 193
Tunnard, W. A., 178
Tupelo (Ms.), 95, 99, 101, 102, 103,
  104, 110, 111, 112, 113, 142
Tupelo Museum, 104
Tupelo National Battlefield, 102,
  104
Turpin Creek Picnic Area, 196,
  201
Tuscumbia (Al.), 55, 56, 58, 59
Twain, Mark, 177, 178
Twentymile Bottom Overlook, 88,
  94
Twentymile Creek, 94

United States Army, 14, 35
United States Army Corps of
  Engineers, 89, 90
United States Congress, 48
United States Forest Service, 100,
  107, 111
Upper Choctaw Boundary, 141,
  147
USS *Cairo*, 181, 182
USS *Mississippi*, 162

Vaughan (Ms.), 142, 143
Velchoff's Corner, 192
Verandah House, 79
Vick, Newit, 182
Vicksburg (Ms.): 161, 168, 173,
  174-85, 188, 189-93, 213
Vicksburg (battle), 168
Vicksburg Convention and
  Visitors Bureau, 182
Vicksburg National Cemetery, 182
Vicksburg National Military Park,
  102, 173, 174, 179, 180, 181,
  182
"Volunteer State," 49

W. C. Handy Home and Museum,
  58